Elmer Kelton

essays and memories

Elmer Kelton

essays and memories

EDITED BY Judy Alter *and* James Ward Lee

TCU Press / *Fort Worth, Texas*

Library of Congress Cataloging-in-Publication Data

Elmer Kelton : essays and memories / [edited by] Judy Alter and James Ward Lee.
p. cm.
Includes bibliographical references.
ISBN 978-0-87565-426-3 (pbk. : alk. paper)
1. Kelton, Elmer—Criticism and interpretation. 2. Western stories—History and
criticism. 3. Texas—In literature. I. Alter, Judy, 1938– II. Lee, James Ward.
PS3561.E3975Z66 2011
813'.54—dc22
2010023248

TCU Press
P. O. Box 298300
Fort Worth, Texas 76129
817.257.7822
http://www.prs.tcu.edu

To order books: 800.826.8911

Illustration and design by Barbara Mathews Whitehead

Contents

Two Careers in One

Judy Alter

An overview of elmer kelton's life and work seems redundant. Those of us who knew and loved him and listened spellbound to speech after speech, often hearing the same stories repeated, feel that we already know about his life and career. But it seems important to set the stage for this book of essays and memories.

Elmer used to tell the story about an old rancher who came up and asked him, "Elmer, did you know there's some fellow out there writing novels and using your name?" The story perfectly illustrates Elmer's dual careers—to the ranching world, he was "one of us," as rancher John Merrill once said to me; in the world of western literature, he stood with the best of our writers, having earned lifetime achievement awards from Western Writers of America, Inc., the Texas Institute of Letters, and the Western Literature Association. He received seven Spur Awards for individual books from Western Writers of America and four Western Heritage Awards from the National Cowboy & Western Heritage Museum. He missed very few WWA conventions in his career and was always a staunch supporter of that organization, always willing to help newcomers or share a beer and talk of old times. When he died in August 2009, WWA members from all over Texas and the American West joined the more than six hundred people who celebrated his life in a service where the anthem was "The Eyes of Texas," and the recessional, "Happy Trails." Noting his passing, *The New York Times* called him the personification of the term "regionalist" and hailed him as the "novelist who brought the sensibility of the old-style western to bear on a modern Texas landscape of oil fields and financially troubled ranches."

In 1997, the Texas Legislature declared Elmer Kelton Day, and in 1998 he received the first Lone Star Award for lifetime achievement from the Larry McMurtry Center for Arts and Humanities at Midwestern University in Wichita Falls, Texas. Honorary degrees came his way from Hardin-Simmons University and Texas Tech University, along with a Lifetime Achievement award from the National Cowboy Symposium held in Lubbock. In addition, he was an honorary member of the German Association for the Study of the Western, which gives an annual Elmer Kelton Award for Literary Merit. (see http://www.westernforschungszentrum.de).

He had his likeness (on horseback) preserved in bronze, met with both Laura and George W. Bush, and has a star in his name in the sidewalk at the Fort Worth Stockyards National Historic District (which he claimed was much more appropriate than a star on a sidewalk in Hollywood). In spite of honors and attention, Elmer remained the most modest and self-deprecating man, a genuine gentleman.

Raised on the McElroy Ranch in Crane and Upton counties in Texas, he was the oldest of four sons of ranch foreman Buck Kelton and his wife, Bea. Elmer grew up knowing ranch life, but in his own words, he "never made a hand." His younger brothers, especially Myrle, were better at roping than he was, and Elmer's idea of watching the herd was to keep one eye on the cattle and the other on the book is his lap.

From a young age, he was a bookish youngster, taught early to read by his mother, whose reading included among other things the pulp magazine *Ranch Romances*, for which Elmer would later write. Because of that he entered school at an advanced grade and was always smaller than his older classmates—and always the last chosen when sides were called to play touch football. With his weak eyes, he couldn't see the ball until it struck him in the face, and he much preferred to sit on the sidelines and watch sports.

Being a cowboy, he has said, is a way of life, and boys were expected to follow in their father's footsteps, but Elmer knew he'd never earn a living that way. He was torn between the two things at which he excelled—writing and drawing. In high school, he studied under the late legendary Texas folklorist Paul Patterson, another bookish kid from a ranch family. He credits Patterson with inspiring him to study journalism.

He was a senior in high school when he told his father he wanted to be a journalist. In a story he repeated often, he said his father gave him a look that "could have killed Johnson grass" and then declared that the trouble with kids in those days was they didn't want to work for a living. His father relented and sent him to the University of Texas, insisting if he wanted to be a journalist, he had to have the best education.

University study was interrupted by service in World War II, from which he returned with his Austrian bride, Ann. He went back to UT and between studies began writing short stories to submit to the pulps, the magazines with lurid covers and violent action on which he had grown up. By the late 1940s, the pulps were dying out but were still a good place for a beginning writer. Elmer used to claim that by the time he returned from posting one in a mailbox, the rejection was waiting in his mailbox.

Finally he submitted a story to Fanny Ellsworth, editor of *Ranch Romances*. Ellsworth tolerated deviation from the western formula: not every story had to have a hero, a villain, and a gunfight. Even though she rejected his first stories, Ellsworth saw possibilities in this writer, and her rejection letters were filled with advice on plotting and characters. The first published Elmer Kelton short story was "There's Always a Second Chance," (1947) in *Ranch Romances*. He received $50 for that story and was sure sales thereafter would come easily, but it was almost a year before he sold a second story and three or four years before he could count on selling most of what he wrote. Over the years he wrote and published many more short stories, and later he would call the early ones amateurish, taking on "the purple hue of the overly melodramatic or the shamelessly sentimental." But he was learning.

His income from writing could not support a growing family, and he worked in agricultural journalism as a livestock and farm writer for the *San Angelo Standard Times* and editor of *Sheep and Goat Raiser Magazine* before settling in to a long career as associate editor and then editor of *Livestock Weekly*. (Fittingly, since cowboys follow in their father's footsteps, son Steve is now editor of the same publication.)

Elmer's first novel was published by Ballantine Books, where Betty Ballantine insisted her writers move away from the traditional western, the pattern set by Owen Wister in *The Virginian*. Elmer would later say he owed a lot of his writing success to women editors. *Hot Iron* was published in1955, and his novels began to move farther from the traditional because of their incorporation of history and their use of more complex characters. Still, Elmer called his early novels "powder burners."

As Elmer continued to write traditional novels, his worked moved slowly toward the six major novels that broke him out of the pulp and powder burner markets. And he was developing his own wry wit and that understated West Texas narrative voice that characterizes the best of his novels. One of his last "traditional" novels was *Dark Thicket* (1985), which, like so much of his work, explores the influence of the Civil War on Texas.

Kelton's move into what some critics call his mature novels came in 1971, with publication of *The Day the Cowboys Quit*. At the same time, encouraged by his longtime literary agent Gus Lenninger, he left Ballantine Books and the world of original paperback novels. Doubleday accepted the 60,000-word *The Day the Cowboys Quit* for its Double D series of westerns, which enjoyed steady library sales but little in the way of popular or critical attention. Editor Harold

Kuebler, who later worked with Elmer for years, suggested that he lengthen the novel by 20,000 words, emphasizing character and de-emphasizing some of the traditional formulaic elements. It was then published as a mainstream trade novel, rather than a Double D Western.

The Day the Cowboys Quit is based on the 1880's cowboy strike at Tascosa, Texas, when individual cowboys clashed with the owners of ranches. More and more small ranchers were being squeezed out by bigger spreads, often owned by eastern corporations. Besides being a darn good story, the novel provides lessons on both history (the disappearance of the old ways of ranch life for cowboys) and agricultural economics. Like many of Kelton's novels it is often used in the classroom.

Five major novels followed: *The Time It Never Rained* (1973); *The Good Old Boys* (1978); The *Wolf and the Buffalo* (1980); *Stand Proud,* (1984); and *The Man Who Rode Midnight* (1987).

The Time It Never Rained may well be Kelton's classic novel. He himself said that though he thought *The Good Old Boys* a close second, but *The Time It Never Rained* is the one of his books he would choose to represent him in a collection of Texas books. Inspired by the seven-year drought of the 1950s, it is a book Kelton labored over, first writing it in the late 1950s, shelving it, and then coming back to rewrite it after the success of *The Day the Cowboys Quit.* Western literature critic Jon Tuska has called it "one of the dozen or so best novels written by an American in [the twentieth] century," and cowboy/author John Erickson wrote, "It is one of the treasures of American literature of any age or time. Our great-grandchildren will be reading Elmer Kelton." Astronaut Rick Sturckow took the novel with him on a manned space mission in 2001.

The Time It Never Rained is the story of one man, Charlie Flagg, and his struggle against the drought. Elmer used to say that while the typical western hero was six feet tall and invincible, his heroes were 5'8" and nervous. Flagg is not necessarily nervous, but neither is he invincible. He's a middle-aged man whose knees are giving him trouble and his belly sags a bit over his belt, but he has built a successful medium-sized ranch. In his foreword Elmer wrote that he hoped the novel would give urban people a better understanding of the difficulties ranchers and farmers face in trying to provide food and clothing for the nation. When I once wrote jacket copy for the TCU Press 1984 reprint, I ended it with a suggestion that Charlie Flagg was a defeated man when the drought finally broke. Elmer protested that he didn't see it that way at all: Charlie Flagg had held true to his character and weathered defeat to emerge as strong as ever.

The prologue contains some of Kelton's most memorable prose:

> *It crept up out of Mexico, touching first along the brackish Pecos and spreading in all directions, a cancerous blight burning a scar on the land.*
>
> *Just another dry spell, men said at first. Ranchers watched waterholes recede to brown puddles of mud that their livestock would not touch. They watched the rank weeds shrivel as the west wind relentlessly sought them out and smothered them with its hot breath. The watched the grass slowly lose its green, then curl and fire up like dying cornstalks. . . .*
>
> *Men grumbled, but you learned to live with the dry spells if you stayed in West Texas; there were more dry spells than wet ones. . . .*
>
> *Why worry? They said. It would rain this fall. It always had.*
>
> *But it didn't. And many a boy would become a man before the land was green again.*

The Good Old Boys is the most personal of Elmer's novels, written at the bedside of his dying father and based on stories he had heard from his father over the years. The first few chapters came slowly, even painfully, but the story suddenly took over. Kelton said it was "like a cold-jawed horse grabbing onto the bit and about all I could do was hang on for the ride." Though he had other experiences with characters taking over novels, this—and *The Wolf and the Buffalo*—are as close as he has come to sheer inspiration. Like many of these major novels, *The Good Old Boys* is about a dying culture, that of the free cowboy life—or the myth that saw cowboy life that way. In spite of many efforts, it is the only novel ever brought to the screen. In 1995, Tommy Lee Jones directed and acted in a made-for-TV movie, along with Cissy Spacek.

The Wolf and the Buffalo turns again to a dying way of life, paralleled by a rising new culture. Kelton intended it to be a book about Gideon Ledbetter, a freed slave who joined the Tenth Cavalry of Buffalo Soldiers. Both Doubleday and *Reader's Digest Condensed Books* wanted a story about the Indian wars and the part of black soldiers from the Buffalo Soldiers' point of view. Kelton resisted, thinking the story should be told by a black man, but his publishers insisted.

As he began to write, the novel soon became the story of a second man—Gray Horse Running, a Comanche. Gray Horse was intended as a minor character, a counterpoint to Gideon, but as Kelton wrote in his introduction,

> *Gray Horse would not let me get away with it . . . A character can grab a story and run off in directions of his own, sometimes against the writer's wishes . . . . Gray Horse kept expanding his role, rivaling the attention given to Gideon. He forced me to take a deeper and more compassionate look at his tragic situation.*

In *Stand Proud*, Elmer varied his usual straightforward narrative pattern to make heavy use of flashback. It is the story of Frank Claymore, a rancher who when young was a hero but as he ages is seen as simply a greedy despot. Kelton suggested that had Claymore not been tough, he never would have survived, let alone built his ranching empire. Still, he is certainly one of Kelton's least likeable heroes. Some critics called the novel, with its structural departure from his usual style and its un-Kelton like surprise ending, evidence of Kelton's continuing maturation as a novelist. It is possible that Elmer had Charlie Goodnight of the Palo Duro Canyon in his mind as he wrote.

Kelton's most contemporary novel is *The Man Who Rode Midnight*, the title being a nod to Midnight, one of the greatest bucking bulls ever, one that few men could stay on for eight seconds. The story focuses on a generational clash between Wes Hendrix, a milder version of Frank Claymore, and his city-bred grandson, Jim Ed Hendrix, who couldn't care less about bull-riding records. Once again, Kelton has crafted a story about a way of life now gone and an old man who has a hard time coming to grips with that.

In between these so-called major novels, Kelton continued to write other books—*Manhunters*, *Wagontongue*. And, under the pseudonym Lee McElroy, he wrote *Joe Pepper* and *Long Way to Texas*, while writing *Shotgun Settlement* as Alex Hawk. He wrote nonfiction—for instance, *Permian: A Continuing Saga* (Midland: Permian Basin Petroleum Museum)—and he was in constant demand to write forewords to other people's work. Several collections of his short stories were published, including *There's Always a Second Chance* (San Angelo, Texas: Fort Concho Museum Press). His text for *The Art of Howard Terpning* won him another Wrangler Award.

In 1990, Kelton retired from the *Livestock Weekly* and devoted himself to his own writing. In the twenty years left to him, he wrote many significant books. *Slaughter*, an account of the destruction of the bison on the high plains, was published by Doubleday in 1992, followed by the sequel *The Far Canyon* (1994). TCU Press, which reprinted many Kelton novels to keep them in print in both hardcover and trade paper editions, came out with the original *Elmer Kelton Country: The Short Nonfiction of a Texas Novelist* (profiles and other pieces he had published over the years in *Livestock Weekly*).

By 1995, both Gus Lenniger and Harold Kuebler had retired, and Elmer found a new agent—Nat Sobel, of Sobel Weber Associates—and a new publisher, TOR/Forge. Over the next years, Elmer produced fourteen novels—seven in the Texas Ranger series, three in the Buckalew Family series, and two more in the Hewey Calloway series. Calloway is the fiddle-footed cowboy who couldn't settle down in *The Good Old Boys*, and Elmer wrote a prequel—*Two Bits a Day*—and a sequel, *The Smiling Country*. TOR/Forge brought back some of his early paperbacks in hard cover, including volumes that included two or more novels: *Brush Country (Barbed Wire* and *Llano River), Texas Showdown (Pecos Crossing* and *Showdown)*, and *Texas Sunrise (Massacre at Goliad* and *After the Bugles)*. TOR/Forge also brought back Kelton's trilogy on Texas independence, originally published under the pen name of Tom Early: *Sons of Texas, The Rebels*, and *The Raiders.*

Elmer Kelton died August 2009 at the age of eighty-three, universally mourned by the western writing community and his many friends and fans throughout the world. He had battled pneumonia most of the summer and was alternately in the hospital and an assisted living community. He remained optimistic about his recovery, and I have heard that the night before he died he was sitting up in bed, talking with friends and jotting down ideas for the next Hewey Calloway novel he planned. He died in his sleep.

The last novel published before his death was *Hard Trail to Follow* (number seven in the Texas Rangers Series). Two novels were published posthumously: *Other Men's Horses* (number eight in the series) and *Texas Standoff* (number nine).

This, then, was Elmer Kelton, a West Texan who wrote about West Texas agriculture and wrote novels about West Texas, using in both arenas the knowledge from his heritage and his childhood. Readers should be grateful that he never made a hand, just as he was always grateful to teachers who, by promoting him too fast, made a bookish person out of him.

Kelton's world of cowboys and cattle is a mixed blessing. It gave him the voice and subject matter to create powerful novels but it cast him into a literary ghetto, since westerns are considered genre fiction and have never earned much respect in this country (Germany seems to value them a lot more). But Elmer Kelton used the American West as a vehicle to study mankind, his strengths, weaknesses, actions, and reactions. Most often he specifically explored the way mankind responds to changing situations, such as the dying cowboy way of life. When the West as a setting is used as an end itself, the result is genre fiction; when it is used to study mankind, it is literature. "Is it," he once asked, "any less valid because I set it in Texas—than if it were in New York or New England or *Old* England?"

When, at the urging of his agent, Kelton wrote an autobiography, *Sandhills Boy: The Winding Trail of a Texas Writer* (2007), he originally wanted to call it *Short in the Saddle* but someone told him readers wouldn't get it. Longtime Kelton friend and fan Dale Walker wrote, "*Short in the Saddle* was Elmer to a tee: the most modest of the best of all western writers and a man with a sly sense of humor. He was a joy to know and to read. I will miss him forever." So will we all.

My Friend Elmer Kelton

Felton Cochran

THE EVENING BEFORE HE PASSED, I had my last conversation with Elmer. I had stopped for a visit with him at the care center where he'd been undergoing rehab for about two months. He was propped up in his hospital bed and as he shook my hand, he admitted to being "a little tired" from his exercise workout that day. His family was present, and after a while our conversation turned to the evolution of his writing career. He told us he remembered he was paid one and a quarter cents per word for his first short stories. "It didn't take long for me to figure that a twenty-thousand word novella was better than a five thousand word short story." He talked about his earliest books published in paperback and how his first two novels—*Hot Iron* and *Buffalo Wagons*—were also issued in a very limited run of hardbacks mainly for library distribution. He mentioned he was paid about $1,500 for those novels, "good money for those days." And he remembered how elated he was when he entered the "big time" when his first major hardback, *The Day the Cowboys Quit*, was published in 1972. He recalled his relationships with his three major publishers, Ballantine, Doubleday, and Forge Press. And how pleased he had been with Forge. It was an engaging and enlightening conversation, with no hint of what was to come early the next morning. As I was leaving, he smiled, waved two fingers at me, and said, "Thanks for coming by, Felton." A few hours later, he died peacefully in his sleep . . .

Elmer Kelton was the quintessential "good old boy" who truly appreciated his many fans. He was always willing, even eager, to sign a stack of books for a fan.

Some folks think he was just another western writer. Some who've never read his works inevitably ask if his books are "like Louis L'Amour's?" They aren't, of course. I tell people Elmer Kelton didn't write "westerns"—he wrote western literature. When you open a Kelton novel, you know beforehand that it will be clean, historically accurate, and entertaining. And somewhere on those pages will be a subtle message. Sounds simple. But his writing was so much more than that. You'll just have to read a Kelton novel to discover what I learned so many years ago.

Regretfully, he didn't live to see the life-size statue of him that will be placed in the new Tom Green County Library sometime next year. His last public appearance was at the "Toast to Elmer Kelton" held in May at the Fort Concho Commissary. It was a catered event and all seats were filled—people showed up from around the state. At that event we presented him and his family with a bronze miniature replica of the statue and a bronze bust of Elmer. At least he died knowing the statue is on its way to completion. And that it is being done by artist Raul Ruiz, who comes from a Tom Green County family that Elmer knew intimately for many years.

One of my life's greatest treasures is a signed copy of the book he had dedicated to me—*Texas Vendetta*. The dedication page of that book reads: "To Felton Cochran, bookseller extraordinaire."

I will always remember him as "friend extraordinaire."

A Eulogy

The Reverend Ricky Burk,
Senior Pastor, First United
Methodist Church of San Angelo

IN HIS AUTOBIOGRAPHY, *Sandhills Boy*, Elmer says he discovered America on April 29, 1926, at Horse Camp on the Five Wells Ranch a few miles east of Andrews, Texas. His mother often told him that it was a wet, stormy day, and the first few weeks were equally stormy for Elmer and his parents. Elmer was born prematurely, and his mother kept him in a shoebox, often in the oven, in order to keep him warm and help him survive those first perilous weeks.

Although he grew up on a ranch, Elmer and horses never connected. He said it might have begun before he was even able to walk. His father was working half-broken horses, and his mom was sitting on the fence holding him and watching her husband. Dad decided it was time for Elmer to have his first ride, so he placed Elmer in front of him in the saddle. The bronc immediately began to pitch while Dad held on to the reins with one hand and Elmer with the other. He calmly worked the bucking bronc around to where Mom was seated on the fence and handed off Elmer like a quarterback handing off a football. Elmer said that from that day forward his relationship with horses went downhill.

The family showed me a picture of the last time Elmer was ever on a horse. He was in the Big Bend area and posed on a big, beautiful palomino for a picture. You can tell by looking at both Elmer and the horse that neither was sure what would happen next. Elmer never mounted a horse again and, years later, when plans were made for the library statue now in progress, he made the artist promise to place him next to a fence, not on a horse!

Growing up in the midst of cowboys and horses, it was always his dream to be a cowboy like his dad. But, in addition to his lack of confidence in riding, he was seriously near-sighted. It often caused him to mess up the cattle drive by getting lost or turned around. But soon Elmer made two great discoveries: glasses and books. He was a voracious reader, immersing himself in any available print.

He missed most of fifth grade due to a mild form of tuberculosis. Forced to stay in bed most of the time, he read, wrote, and did imaginary radio broadcasts. He even made his own movies by drawing pictures on long strips of paper, then pulling them through slots in a large piece of cardboard, one at a time. From behind the cardboard he would voice the dialogue. His God-given gift was beginning to surface.

As he faced graduation from high school he began to work up the nerve to break the news to his father about his intended career. Elmer finally told him that he wanted to go to the University of Texas, study journalism, and become a writer. His dad, a hard-core rancher to the bone, didn't take it well. Elmer said, "He gave me a look that would kill Johnson grass and said, 'That's the problem with you kids these days, you all want to make a living without working for it.'" Elmer was never certain what his father thought about his career.

Soon the drums of war began to beat in Europe and Elmer decided to do his part and enlist in the navy. They turned him down due to flat feet. That was no problem for the army and when he turned eighteen they accepted him. His basic training was at Fort Bliss, near El Paso. He graduated around Christmas and was given holiday leave to a base near Gainesville, Texas. It was there he began to attend a Methodist Church. He was given a New Testament, which he carried overseas and always kept in his pocket. Shortly before he shipped out he attended a service that concluded with the hymn "Just as I Am." He said the words burned into his memory and brought him comfort during the many difficult times ahead.

Once as I visited Elmer in the nursing home I felt the need, as his pastor, to ask about his relationship with God. Had he made peace with God? Did he have the assurance of his salvation? Although he was lying flat on his back, he propped himself up on both elbows, looked me straight in the eye and said, "Oh yes, Preacher. I took care of that a long time ago." I've always wondered if that commitment was made at that Methodist church service as he listened to the words of "Just as I Am."

During the war Elmer was dispatched to the little Austrian town of Ebensee. There he would meet the love of his life, his wife for sixty-two years, Anni Lipp. In *Sandhills Boy* he says, "the course of one's life may hinge on a chance moment, an unanticipated coincidence. It was by pure chance that I happened to be at Ebensee's boat landing the evening of October 14, 1945, and met Anni Lipp. She had a little boy named Gerhard, then four-going-on-five and without a father. By the time the relationship became serious I was deeply attached to him." Anni would always lovingly say that Elmer was like a stray pet, "I fed a soldier apple strudel and he kept coming back."

But soon the war was over and Elmer was sent back stateside. He promised that he would return for Anni and Gerhard. Every day, for more than a year, he wrote her a letter. Anni said that she could read very little English but it didn't matter because each letter meant that he would keep his promise and return for them.

Elmer finally fought his way through the red tape of government beauracracy and brought Anni and little Gerhard home to Texas. They were married in his grandmother's house in Midland. There was no honeymoon, only work to be done. About a week after her arrival, Elmer took Anni to Pecos to introduce her to the thrill of a rodeo. It was hot, dusty, windy, and a far cry from the beauty of Austria. She's never been to a Pecos rodeo since.

Little Gerhard adjusted quickly. He picked up English easily from the cowboys. The only problem was that most of them were four-letter words he couldn't repeat! The cowboys decided that Gerhard was too foreign-sounding so they began calling him Gary for short, and Gary it still is.

Elmer, Anni, and Gary soon moved to San Angelo and he began working for the *San Angelo Standard-Times*. That was his day job. At night he would work on his writings, slowly enjoying success. He would eventually write over sixty books (two will come out in the near future) including *The Time It Never Rained*, *The Good Old Boys*, which Tommy Lee Jones turned into a movie, *The Wolf and the Buffalo*, *The Day the Cowboys Quit*, *The Man Who Road Midnight*, and many others I'm sure you would call your favorite.

Through the characters of his writings Elmer taught us a lot about life. His books were about basic human nature, the struggles we all face. In *Sandhills Boy* he wrote, "I try to avoid superheroes, for I have never known any. The people I have known have for the most part been common folks struggling to get along, meeting life's obstacles with the best that is in them, or in some cases giving up and going down in defeat. Not all stories have a happy ending. Life is not that kind to us."

In *The Time It Never Rained* he wrote concerning his characters:

> *They are not the traditional Western fictional heroes, standing up to a villain for one splendid moment of glory. They are quiet but determined men and women who stand their ground year after year in a fight they can never fully win, against an unforgiving enemy they know will return to challenge them again and again so long as they live. They are the true heroes.*

In *The Good Old Boys* he writes about Hewey Calloway, (his favorite character) stating:

Hewey, like all of us, faces the necessity of painful choices, knowing that every choice will bring sacrifices. He knows, as we all know, that we cannot have everything we want in this life. To fulfill a wish we often must give up something of equal or nearly equal value. He cannot have it all; nobody can. In this respect, Hewey Calloway is all of us.

To read Elmer Kelton is to understand the world itself. He recognized the human dilemma as few of us do and articulated its reality with such clarity that anyone could learn from him. He was one of life's greatest teachers.

Elmer was named the greatest western writer of all time by the Western Writers of America. Seven times he was awarded the Spur Award for the best novel of the year. He received four Western Heritage Awards from the National Cowboy & Western Heritage Museum, and countless awards and recognitions too numerous to list.

Yet, Elmer always said his proudest moment was when he broke the story about Billie Sol Estes to the national press in the early sixties. The Estes scandal shook the Pecos area like an earthquake, triggering a rash of bankruptcies, at least a couple of violent deaths, the derailing of political careers, and a prison sentence for Estes.

At one point it was rumored that Estes had fled the country. Estes' attorney wanted to put that rumor to rest and decided to choose two journalists—out of hundreds—to accompany him to his hotel room where Estes was staying. One of the chosen was Elmer Kelton. Elmer wrote repeated articles about the Estes scandal and always felt it was then that he did his best work *because both sides were mad at him!*

As it has already been stated, history will record that Elmer didn't write westerns—he wrote western literature. When you opened a Kelton novel you knew it would be clean enough for any member of the family to read, always historically accurate, and inspirational. His readers loved him—a gentle, unassuming, humble man always willing to talk to anyone, sign a stack of books, or offer advice to would-be writers.

And, I believe that history will also record that even though he was a great writer, he was even greater in character. To rub shoulders with Elmer Kelton made you want to be a better person and leave this world better than you found it. I will never cease to be amazed how he could achieve such fame, popularity, and, no doubt, the wealth that came with it, yet never let it change him. In a world where success is harder to handle than failure, Elmer remained untouched.

Elmer Kelton. Today we say good-bye to one of the giants in literature. He has changed our lives and made our world better. Although he has left us, we are left with the treasures of his writings.

Journalism's Influence on Elmer Kelton's Fiction

4

Steve Kelton

I KNEW ELMER KELTON for almost sixty years, exactly a month shy of fifty-eight, to be precise, though the first few of those years are a little sketchy. He was my dad, so with your indulgence, that's how I will refer to him here. It would feel a bit awkward to call him Elmer, and he always insisted that *Mr. Kelton* was *his* father, my grandfather.

As far back as I can recall, he worked at a newspaper during the day and at his own typewriter at night. More than once in later years, he expressed regret that perhaps he hadn't given us kids as much attention as other fathers gave to their children, hammering away at that typewriter from shortly after supper until long after we'd gone to bed. But for us, that was normal; we didn't know any different, and if we lacked for attention, we were unaware of it.

Dad's day job paid the bills, and all that hammering and clattering at night allowed for a few extras. Only a handful of people have ever become wealthy writing for a newspaper, and Dad didn't break that mold. From 1948 until well into 1990, he worked full-time, first for the *San Angelo Standard-Times*, then from 1963 until 1968 for the *Sheep & Goat Raiser* magazine, and the final twenty-two years for *Livestock Weekly*.

He often said that the two separate careers complemented one another. Writing fiction gave him an outlet for his imagination and allowed him to indulge a need to explore his subject in greater depth than was possible in a straight news format, not to mention the freedom to express opinions. Many if not most of today's newspaper reporters appear not to have heard of that last limitation, but for Dad it was sacrosanct.

His journalistic work, on the other hand, taught him the discipline of deadlines—I doubt he ever missed any—and ingrained a certain discipline in his wordsmithing, as well. His prose never rambled or became self-indulgent, and he seldom used five words where three would do. Perhaps most important were the contacts he made as a reporter, the people he met and the stories he heard.

Some of the people he interviewed were old-timers in their own right fifty or sixty years ago and provided living links to the periods and places in which his stories would be set. Others had known such old-timers or recounted family stories passed down through the generations. Together they peopled his novels, at least in bits and pieces, and gave flesh and context to his own extensive study of history.

Just as he was careful not to color his "straight" reporting with his own opinions and attitudes, Dad believed that people of other times should not be judged by the opinions and attitudes of today. They may have done, said, and thought things that offend the sensibilities of modern political correctness, but they lived in a different and usually much harsher reality. That reality would gobble up a transplanted modern moralist before he or she could finish wagging a finger.

Dad was always careful in his settings; he had been to the places he wrote about. There were no stands of saguaro cactus in his West Texas fiction, just as there were no saguaro cactus in the real West Texas he wrote about. His day job gave him the opportunity to travel to those places as he pursued the stories he wrote for the publications that paid his salary. This was especially true at *Livestock Weekly*, where stories were seldom assigned, and he had the freedom as well as responsibility to seek out his own material. If he wanted to stand on the ground where the battle of San Jacinto was fought, he found a story in that vicinity. If he needed to absorb the atmosphere of the last buffalo hunts or the battle of Adobe Walls, there was a feedlot in the Texas Panhandle doing something new or different. All of those experiences found their way into his books at one time or another and gave them the authenticity that readers recognized, appreciated, and trusted.

Many of the myriad factual elements that gave his books their flavor were fragmentary and identifiable only in the aggregate, but he could and did point to a few individual stories that were transported relatively intact. Dad spoke to many diverse groups, from the Texas Folklore Society to local chambers of commerce and groups of school children. One of those talks, a 1988 address to the Folklore Society, took a humorous look at fiction writing in general and his own work in particular. Roughly paraphrasing, he said that someone who incorporates the words of another into his own is a plagiarist; one who incorporates the words of a few is a researcher; and one who incorporates the words of many is a fiction writer. Fiction is by definition untrue; therefore, fiction writers are both liars and thieves.

One of the stories he openly admitted "stealing" helped him flesh out a character in his first "serious" western, *The Day the Cowboys Quit.* It was a fictional treatment of a true-life cowboy strike in the Panhandle in the 1880s. Among the lesser characters but critical to the plot was a cold-blooded gunslinger hired by a syndicate of big Eastern-financed ranches to stop what they condemned as rustling but what most of their targets regarded as a legitimate effort to graze a few small herds on untitled state land that the big outfits held by dint of seniority and, later, by force. The gunfighter was real—you probably all know the name Pat Garrett—as was the conflict.

Dad had a problem with his fictional gunslinger, however. The man was based on the real Garrett but wasn't realistic—there was no humanity to him—and Dad was never comfortable with two-dimensional, cardboard characters, good or bad. The reader needed some reason to care about a character, at least a little. Dad found his humanizing element while interviewing an elderly woman named Rachel Bingham at Spur, Texas. She told a true story from her youth in which an aging gunfighter was hired to put down rustling, largely by reputation. He ended up killing a local cowboy—all within the law, as was often the case. Bingham's husband had been a friend of the cowboy, and, disturbed that the lonely grave was repeatedly trampled by cattle and the crude headboard knocked down, decided to fence the plot.

Along the way he encountered the gunslinger who inquired as to his intentions. Al Bingham swallowed hard and told the truth, nervously counting what he feared might be his last breaths. After a pause for reflection, the gunslinger said, "That's a good idea. I'll go help you."

Dad used that story with little modification, and it made his gunslinger realistic as well as real. He became a human being after all, maybe not admirable, but recognizably human.

"I really cared, then, what happened to him," Dad wrote in a 1995 compilation of short non-fiction work. "At the end of the book, when he rides off to die in some distant place, a man who has out-lived his own time and doesn't know it, I felt for him. He had be-come as real as if I had actually known him."

Dad's fictional gunfighter ended up being cheated by the ranch-ers who had hired him. On his way out of the country he got retribu-tion many times over by lighting a range fire that consumed critical fall and winter grazing over a vast swath of land. Readers—this one, anyway—felt the man's sense of betrayal and cheered at least a little when he took his revenge.

That wouldn't have happened had Dad not interviewed Rachel Bingham for a newspaper article.

Another newspaper interview provided the germ of a story that eventually became *Stand Proud*. Many years ago, Dad was inter-viewing an old-timer by the name of Ira Bird in Coke County. Dur-ing the visit, Bird told him a tale of his father, who was a boy during the Civil War. Too young to join the fighting back East, he took up with one of the frontier battalions fighting Indians. On a scout one morning, he crested a hill and looked out across a broad valley black with thousands of buffalo. It was a beautiful sight, and one he never forgot. Later he found his way back, settled there, and left descendants who are there to this day.

The lead character in Dad's book, a hard-bitten, stubborn and unyielding survivor named Frank Claymore, was patterned to some degree on Charles Goodnight, himself a frontier ranger in his youth. The land, however, was Yellow Wolf Valley in Coke County. Dad could write convincingly of its discovery because he heard the story from Ira Bird, and he could describe the land confidently because he'd seen it with his own eyes.

In much the same vein, Dad's job at the *Livestock Weekly* helped him visualize ranch homes, barns, and outbuildings that have added to the authenticity of his fiction writing. He saw many of them during visits as he conducted interviews, and he saw some true classics as he covered the beginning and the growth of the Ranching Heritage Center at Lubbock. The center houses a wealth of historic ranch structures donated by their owners so that they might be preserved and maintained for posterity. Each building was painstakingly disassembled, hauled, and reassembled on the center's sprawling grounds, and Dad wrote about many of the acquisitions as they came in over the years. He seldom if ever described a building in a novel in such detail that it might be recognized, but he knew how the doors swung, how the rooms laid out, whether a barn had a hay loft or feed bins. His characters could negotiate the terrain because Dad could walk them through it in his mind's eye; at no time would they exit the second door on the left if they'd entered through the first.

Because of the time frame for most of his novels, Dad's journalism career naturally impacted his fiction in a mostly indirect manner. He did write a few contemporary stories, however, and these show a more direct connection. One of those was *The Man Who Rode Midnight*. His publisher at the time had suggested that he write a novel with an "environmental" angle. Dad was leery of the idea, mentioning in correspondence with his agent that his own take on "environmental" issues might not be exactly what the New York publisher had in mind.

He had seen the environment up close and personal and had spent a lifetime among people for whom the environment was both a challenge and their future, as well as the future of their children and grandchildren—or so most hoped. They knew it not from books and theories but in all its sometimes harsh realities. The vast majority struggled to make a living from the land and to leave it at least a little better than they had found it. Urbanites many generations removed tended to view the land as they imagined it to be and to dismiss the inhabitants of "flyover country" as usurpers and despoilers of an Eden that had never really existed.

Dad eventually found the underlying conflict he needed for that book in a situation unfolding near San Angelo. A man-made reservoir planned for the Colorado River would supply water for several towns and cities, as well as recreation for their inhabitants. In the process, it would inundate many thousands of acres of ranch and farmland belonging to individuals whose grandparents and great-grandparents had settled the area. It would also swallow the remnants of a once-thriving community that had gradually faded to little more than a post office and store.

Dad moved the location and changed most of the details. The town in his book was not so far along in its decay and was not in the intended lakebed. For the fictional townfolk, the lake was a blessing instead of a curse, perhaps their only hope for revitalization. For his rancher protagonist, however, its suffocating waters would destroy everything he had spent a long life building. He was determined to hold out even as his neighbors accepted what was almost inevitable and sold out for the best price they could get.

The Man Who Rode Midnight involved not only environmental issues, love of the land, and a deep reverence for heritage, but also touched on changes in culture and values. The determined stand of the aging Wes Hendricks turned old friends against him and made enemies of those in town who had never been his friends.

In similar situations, Dad the journalist had seen desperate land-owners ally themselves with environmental activist groups who op-posed such developments for their own reasons and in a different situation would have—and did and still do—try their best to run the ranchers themselves off the same land. Dad toyed with that idea as a plot device but decided against it. It was a Faustian bargain and seldom turned out well. He also dismissed any notion of having Wes Hendricks prevail in the end; that would have been fantasy as much as fiction. And he steered away from the lengthy legal battles that can tie such projects up for decades, which is what happened in so many cases including the reservoir east of San Angelo. Dad was not Erle Stanley Gardner, and the law was a thicket into which he chose not to venture.

Wes Hendricks lost his battle in the end but in waging it gained something of great value that he had never hoped to have. He also retained his dignity and self-respect, key elements of all of Dad's protagonists.

A quasi-contemporary novel, *Honor at Daybreak*, benefited from Dad's journalistic work as well. It was set in the Permian Basin of West Texas during that region's great oil boom beginning in the 1920s. Dad didn't cover the "oil beat" per se, but he met countless ranchers whose own operations or those of their parents were res-cued from the receivers by a timely oil lease bonus and/or depend-able royalty checks.

He also sat only a few feet away from the "oil desk" at the *Standard-Times*. For decades, the *Standard* was an authoritative source for developments in the oil patch, its reporters trusted and respected by the majors and shoestring wildcatters alike. Dad came to know landmen, drillers, oilfield supply people, and independent operators, many of whom had started out as roughnecks in the early boom period. Years later, a few of those still living helped him with the flavor and the details of his story, which also owed much to the recollections of uncles and cousins on his mother's side of the family and to his own experiences growing up as a ranch kid on the edge of several sizeable oil fields.

Without question, the single work that most closely tied Dad's journalism career to his fiction writing was *The Time It Never Rained*. It was the story of the 1950s drouth in West Texas. Depending upon precisely where it was measured, it lasted roughly seven years, a little longer here, a little shorter there. The area has seen longer drouths and some that have been more severe, but the drouth of the 1950s combined the worst elements of length and severity. It was also more deeply felt than later spells because so much of the region's economy was tied to agriculture. When crops and pasture failed, everyone felt it, and fail they did, year after year. It was also particularly difficult because, in those days, it was rare to find a rancher or farmer with a job in town that could help buy the groceries. It's never been so since.

Dad has described that period as one of the two most traumatic experiences in his life; the other was World War II. As an ag reporter for the *Standard-Times*, he covered it day in and day out. He knew the people who were suffering, and he knew them a whole lot better by the time it was over. One night, when the paper was short-handed, he was drafted to fill in as an opera critic. He never said so, but I suspect he considered it a relief.

"I'd long since run out of new ways to say 'dry,'" Dad later remarked.

Long before it was over, he realized he had more than enough material to write a book about it and thus began *The Time It Never Rained*. It took almost three times as long to sell that book as the drouth itself actually lasted. New York publishers simply weren't interested in a novel about a West Texas drouth. Had it been set in Ethiopia, perhaps . . . . To be charitable, the typical easterner had no real frame of reference for such a situation, whether he occupied an office on publisher's row or milked dairy cows in Vermont

or Wisconsin. One of Dad's favorite stories from the era involved a
conversation he had at the stockyards with a lamb buyer from the
Midwest. The buyer was attempting to commiserate.

"It's been awfully dry at home, too," he said. "We've had three
drouths so far this year."

"Sorry to hear that," Dad quipped. "We've had to make do with
the same drouth for three years." He had no way of knowing it wasn't
yet half over.

The book was finally published in 1973, after two complete re-
writes. Dad later observed that the delay and all the extra work were
probably worth it in the end, because the version he ended up with
was much better than the one he'd started out with. Had this and
other fiction been Dad's only source of income, we would all have
starved to death years before, hence his stock advice to aspiring writers: Don't give up your day job.

The lead character is Charlie Flagg, a West Texas rancher a little past middle age. His wasn't a big operation but respectable, and
what he had he'd earned with his own sweat and effort. He would
never accept a handout, and no one would tell him what to do.
That set up one of the primary conflicts in the story; as the severity
of the slow-moving disaster finally made itself known in Washington, the government began to respond with relief efforts. Charlie
Flagg would have nothing to do with those, an unbending position
that not only made life harder than it might have been but strained
relationships with friends and family who came to resent him for
demonstrating a strength of character that they couldn't muster but
wished they had.

The combination of the programs themselves and Charlie's
refusal to participate sometimes had a doubly damaging effect on his
fortunes, as they did in real life to the ranchers who followed Charlie's path. And the ranchers weren't the only ones. A classic example
was the drouth feed subsidy. The theory was simple: USDA would
cut checks to stockmen to help them cope with the rising price of

feed and their ever-increasing need for more of it, "X" number of dollars per ton of feed they purchased. How could that possibly go wrong?

Any reasonably bright student in a high school civics class could guess that as soon as a ten-dollar per ton subsidy was announced, the price of feed would suddenly rise by ten dollars, or maybe twelve. The political class, however, was much too intelligent to put any stock in common sense. Ranchers who received the subsidy saw no net benefit, and for the Charlie Flaggs among them who refused the $10, the price-inflating subsidies provided another bleeding wound.

Local feed stores usually had little control over the prices they paid for the products they resold; that was determined elsewhere. And many of those local dealers soon found themselves up to their necks in the second consequence of Washington's rush to "help." In the interest of getting relief to the countryside as soon as possible, USDA bureaucrats encouraged dealers to sell the feed first and worry about the details later. It would be months before regulations were written to govern the process. When those rules finally emerged, feed companies across the region found themselves in criminal violation of chapters, sections, and paragraphs that hadn't been written when the deeds were done. The lucky ones simply didn't get paid.

Dad saw that debacle unfold, and that, along with his wartime experiences, confirmed his suspicions that government not only didn't have the answers, it seldom knew the questions.

Other difficulties arose with the "bracero" guest-worker program whereby a limited amount of labor could be imported from Mexico for agricultural jobs that were becoming harder to fill. World War II had drastically reduced the agricultural labor force as Uncle Sam drained men from all private sectors and put them in uniform. When the war ended, millions gladly returned to their previous pursuits and even created a temporary glut as they reintegrated into private life. There was no glut of cowboys and ranch hands, however. These men had seen the lights of the city, and those lights were seductive even under blackouts. The returning GIs also wanted to marry and start families; the long-running tradition of the bachelor cowboy was over, and few ranches had or could afford facilities to house family men.

The bracero program proved a poor substitute. Unlike fruit and vegetable harvests, ranch work did not lend itself to unskilled labor. The rules and regulations were also unworkable, having been conjured up by bureaucrats with no concept of how real life worked. Dad wrote about the emerging plan in considerable detail at the *Standard-Times*, and his background preparations even included a lengthy trip into the interior of Mexico. There he saw braceros recruited by the busload, and was able to contrast the living conditions common to them with what Washington insisted must be provided north of the Bravo. One of his favorite Ace Reid cartoons showed the exasperated rancher trying to convince his guest worker to get up from the bunkhouse floor. "I don't care how you do it back home," he argued, "the government says you have to sleep in a bed!"

Beyond what limited direct impact the program had on ranchers, it significantly increased the presence of the border patrol in West Texas. Mexican nationals had been cowboying on some Texas ranches for decades, even generations. Their legal status had seldom been an issue because few outside the region had ever been aware of it. Even veteran border patrol agents often looked the other way or made their own separate peace with a situation that worked well for all involved. It was no threat to the AFL-CIO. As the agency expanded to take on enforcement of the bracero program, however, considerable numbers of new personnel came in, and they knew nothing and cared less about the old ways. That was one of many threads that wove their way through *The Time It Never Rained*.

The published version of the book treated all these issues somewhat obliquely, and for good reason. Dad once told my mother that one of the reasons his original version had been rejected was because its politics were unwelcome back east. Evidently, government programs were to be judged on their good intentions, not their sometimes disastrous results. Political correctness is clearly not a new phenomenon. The ill effects of such programs played a large role in the miseries of the 1950s drouth, however, and the story could not be told honestly or completely without acknowledging that fact. Dad just had to learn how to be sneaky about it. He did that by showing the effects on his characters, and characters were always his strong suit. It undoubtedly made for a much better book.

Charlie Flagg, of course, was the central character, but Dad created a large and diverse cast, all of them drawn in one way or another from people he came to know as he traveled and reported agricultural stories on a daily basis. Almost all of them were composites, a little of this person, a little of that, a pinch of the fellow over there. He dedicated the book to my grandfather and openly credited much of Charlie Flagg's character to him. My grandmother was convinced that he *was* Charlie Flagg. Others were equally convinced that Charlie was their husband, father, uncle, or grandfather, and as Dad said more than once, they were all right.

Some characters had a much more limited gene pool. Charlie's best friend, Page Mauldin, is one. A central character, Mauldin is a go-getter, an ambitious and hard-working man who aspires to be the biggest rancher in West Texas and is well on his way when the drouth sets in. To get that big, he has leveraged just about everything he owns, and when Mother Nature closes the tap, it all comes apart. In the end, he loses everything. Dad based Mauldin almost entirely on a single operator, a man he knew well. Because the character was so closely drawn, Dad was afraid the prototype for Mauldin would recognize himself in the book.

"I didn't see how he could possibly miss the connection if he read it," Dad told the Texas Folklore Society in 1988. "One day I ran into him at the San Angelo auction," he continued. "He said, 'I just read your book.' I thought, 'Oh God, here it comes.'"

Instead, Page Mauldin's one-man inspiration said, "You know, I sure did enjoy it. That old Charlie Flagg was just like me!"

"You can believe I never told him any differently," Dad said.

I've saved the end of the book for last, which, I suppose, is appropriate. Fair warning to anyone who hasn't read the book and intends to: what follows is a serious spoiler.

Dad often said of his father that he never owned a pair of rose-colored glasses. Granddad was a natural storyteller, and he had his own way of doing so. I remember him once reminiscing about a man he'd met in 1906, when he was just a little boy. Something about the experience stuck with him, and he described the setting and situation in great detail. The man was riding a sorrel horse with three white stockings, a particular brand on his hip, and a certain way of moving that greatly impressed Granddad. What didn't impress him was anything about the rider. "For the life of me, I can't remember his name or what he looked like."

Most of Granddad's stories were more complete than that. He told fond tales of ranches where he had cowboyed as a young man and of other large outfits he knew of in West Texas. The end of his stories was usually the same: That one went to the receivers in 1929; this one went back to the bank; and another went on the block. None of Granddad's stories ended with happily ever after.

Neither did *The Time It Never Rained*.

By the end of the drouth, Charlie Flagg has lost much of his land and been forced to sell off most of his livestock. All he has left is a nucleus herd of Angora goats from which he plans to rebuild. What happens next is a product of Dad's raising and his experience as a reporter. A predecessor at the *Standard-Times* was a man by the name of Sam Ashburn. Dad and other ag reporters at the paper traded on Ashburn's reputation until they could establish their own. Dad spent some time in the "morgue," the newspaper's archive section, studying the work of Ashburn and others. In the process he came upon a story by Ashburn that told of a friend's tragic experience at the end of the 1930s Dust Bowl drouth. It was the way he wanted to end *The Time It Never Rained*.

Ashburn was long dead, as were the principals in the story. Dad looked up Ashburn's widow and asked her permission to use the tale in his book. She was thrilled that someone remembered her late husband.

In the book, as in real life, Charlie Flagg has just shorn his goats for the mohair that made them valuable. A fresh-shorn Angora is almost helpless against the elements, and even a warm rain can chill them. Charlie has provided low sheds for protection, but Angora goats have never qualified for membership in Mensa. The first drouth-breaking rain catches Charlie's goats in the open, and they are chilled before Charlie and his hand can drive them to shelter. They bunch up, pile up, and begin dying. First a few, then dozens, then scores.

In desperation, Charlie pours gasoline on a pile of dead brush and coaxes a fire out of the wet wood. It grows into a blaze, and some of the struggling goats sense the warmth and begin drifting toward the burning pile. Soon there are others, and then, to Charlie's horror, those in the rear surge forward, forcing those nearest the fire into the flames. The death moans of freezing goats are drowned out by the piercing screams of those being burned alive.

By then Charlie's wife, Mary, has arrived. Together they stare helplessly at the carnage.

"There's still the land," Charlie finally tells her. "A man can always start again. A *man* always *has* to."

No, Dad never owned a pair of rose-colored glasses, but he tried three times before he finally sold the book that would be his signature work. He just wouldn't give up. Charlie Flagg would have understood.

"Hang and Rattle": Change and Endurance in *The Time It Never Rained*

Ruth McAdams

ELMER KELTON SETS *The Time It Never Rained* in the country he knows best during the famous drought that burned up West Texas from 1950 to 1957. Those were seven remarkable years, but there is no doubt that Kelton's part of Texas has always been dry country. As he says in *Living and Writing in West Texas*, drought is "a steady boarder who may stray for a little while but always comes home for supper." The rains, which bring temporary prosperity, he likens to "a flirtatious stranger who occasionally waves but never pauses long enough for a first-name acquaintanceship" (32). Of course Kelton knows that sometimes rains come, even during a drought. But occasional rains during a drought only torment the ranchers. These rains never last long enough to soak into the ground but instead merely bounce off the impenetrable soil like water droplets on a hot griddle. Therefore, "moisture from one [rainfall] seldom remains until the next" (Kelton, Introduction to *The Time It Never Rained* x).

Kelton knew the 1950–1957 drought—or "drouth" as he calls it in the novel—firsthand: "As a farm and ranch reporter I covered that drought day after day for seven years. I ran out of new ways to say, 'It's still dry out there'" (Kelton, *Sandhills Boy* 205). Once his editor at the *San Angelo Standard-Times* even suggested, in an attempt at finding a fresh angle for the drought, that Kelton "go to Fairmount

Cemetery and ask the grave diggers how far it was down to wet dirt" (*Sandhills Boy* 200). Elmer Kelton says his prolonged assignment as a journalist made it possible to write *The Time It Never Rained* (http://www.frontporchrepublic.com/2009/08/elmer-kelton-rip/).

The drought ended in January of 1957, shortly after President Dwight D. Eisenhower toured blighted West Texas, causing residents to rejoice in what they took to calling the "nice Republican rains" (*Sandhills Boy* 206). Kelton began work on the novel shortly after. By this time he had already achieved modest success in the pulp western market, so he sent the novel to his agent, sure it would find a home. It did not. Labeling the work "a nice little agrarian novel" his agent and several publishers' readers did not react favorably (*Sandhills Boy* 206). He completely rewrote the novel. His agent and editors were still not interested, so he tucked the manuscript away in a drawer, never forgetting his "aborted drought novel" (*Sandhills Boy* 207). Time passed, and after critical acceptance of his first "literary" novel, *The Day the Cowboys Quit* in 1971, he completely rewrote *The Time It Never Rained* for a third time, starting from page one. This time it worked, and one of his greatest sources of pride is that "Doubleday published it unedited—'No one ever changed a word,' he says" (Anne Dingus, *Texas Monthly*, Dec. 1995). First published in 1973, the book garnered a Spur Award from the Western Writers of America and the Western Heritage Award from the National Cowboy & Western Heritage Museum in Oklahoma City, as well as critical acclaim, culminating in Jon Tuska's 1982 declaration that it is "'One of the dozen or so best novels written by an American in this century'" (Pilkington, Afterword to *Time* 377).

Kelton himself considers *The Time It Never Rained* the favorite of his works. In an interview with Gary Kent in *Conversations With Texas Writers*, he explains why: "It was more personal to me because in a sense it was more of a reporting job than it was fiction, although I fictionalized the characters. Just about everything that happens in that book, it happened to people I knew about. Very little of the consequences of the drought in that book was not real to me; in other words, I'd seen it happen to someone" (198). In spite of many other novels, and countless articles, speeches, and other publications, the novel remains what Kelton called his "signature work. After more than twenty years, I am more often than not introduced as the author of that book, though I have written many others since" (*Sandhills Boy* 207).

The situation in *The Time It Never Rained* is of course the drought and the price it exacts from its entire cast of characters. Set against a backdrop of history and the West Texas drought, Kelton illuminates two basic themes in *The Time It Never Rained*, the theme of the inevitability of change, and, in the face of such change, the value of endurance. He gets at these ideas through a rich cast of characters in conflict with themselves, other individuals, and clusters of people.

Kelton has written extensively about change as theme in his novels. A particularly cogent example comes from *Living and Writing in West Texas*, as he explains:

> *I usually try to find periods of change for a stage. The history of Texas and the United States has been one of constant change. At any given time you can find the old going out and the new coming in. So you have natural grounds for conflict between the old trying to hold back and the new trying to bring something different . . . each convinced that it is right.* (13)

The conflict, then, comes in knowing when to go along to get along and when to "hang and rattle."

The central character of the novel, Charlie Flagg, best embodies the exigencies of change, a man repeatedly brought up short, confronted with a world not of his making, not of his choosing. Based on Kelton's own rancher father and a whole host of other ranchers, all invested with a sense of cussed independence in the face of "an old frontier ethic of self-sufficiency which a modern society has decided is outmoded," Flagg finds himself time and again out of step with the world around him, alternately bewildered, enraged, and beaten down (Kelton, "The Western and the Literary Ghetto," in *The Texas Literary Tradition*, ed. by Don Graham, James W. Lee, and William T. Pilkington 93). He longs for the good old days throughout the novel, and, like all of us, conveniently forgets the old days were not always all that good. But they are to Charlie, for he still reflects on the "exhilaration in the chase, the spurring and yelling and smashing through brush, the swinging of the rope and bringing those wild cattle crashing to earth" (*Time* 17). Similarly, he fondly recalls the old days with Page Mauldin:

> *They had worked together when Charlie was a big button and Page a cowboy in his twenties. They had ridden broncs together for twenty dollars a month and roped wild cattle out of the thickets and slept on the same blanket under the prairie stars, at a time when the buffalo-grass turf still knew the bite of wagonwheels more than the crush of pneumatic tires. Those had been the good days, the young days, when five dollars in his pocket made a cowboy feel rich as a packinghouse owner. (Time 50)*

Change comes in many ways in the novel, none more forcefully that the ethnic relations that form a part of Charlie's story, especially the young pitted against the old. Charlie Flagg is the most vocal, visible Anglo representation of how the old order relates to both the Texas-Mexican characters and the *mojados*—the ragtag men entering the United States illegally hunting for work and a better life for themselves and their families. In an interview with Patrick Bennett in *Talking With Texas Writers*, Kelton says,

> *Of course, with Charlie Flagg I was trying to tell something about the more or less modern racial thing, and how it had developed to that point, between the Mexican and Anglo people. If you do a story about the ranch country in this part*

*of the world, that's just part of the life. If you ignore it, pre-
tend it doesn't exist, you're not being true to the subject. (190)*

We learn early on that Charlie is solidly entrenched in the pa-
ternalistic system of West Texas when Page Mauldin's hired help, a
"dark-skinned Mexican of forty or more" calls him "Mister Charlie,"
in deference to "an ancient pattern of racial relationships" (*Time*
19). And even though Charlie recognizes it as a dying custom he
admits, "Archaic or not, he sort of liked it" (*Time* 20). Similarly,
Charlie has chosen as his own hired help Lupe Flores, and each
man seems reasonably at ease with a system in which the Anglo is
always in charge:

> *He had always been this way, agreeable to anything
> Charlie said, dependable but never self-asserting. Some
> Mexicans—especially the younger ones—gave Charlie an
> uncomfortable feeling that they were saying one thing in
> agreeing with him while something altogether different was
> going on behind those black eyes. He had latched onto Lupe
> years ago because he had not seen that quality of resistance
> in him. Whatever Charlie wanted always seemed to suit him
> fine; there was never any argument or sign that Lupe even
> considered one. He was comfortably subservient, every ranch
> owner's ideal for a hired man. (Time 21)*

In such a system it is inevitable that Charlie feels responsible for
Lupe and his family. When Danny Ortiz mistreats and nearly rapes
Anita Flores, Charlie is overcome by rage and declares his intention
of going to the sheriff, but Lupe says, "What do you think the sheriff
will say? He will say she is just a Mexican girl out with a Mexican
boy, and that's the way it is with Mexicans" (*Time* 184–85). Charlie
realizes if he did not know Anita personally, she would be "just another Mexican" to him as well. Further, when Lupe's son Manuel
makes threats against Danny, Charlie forbids it and tells him, "You

and your folks are my responsibility, boy. I've always taken care of you. I'll take care of you now" (*Time* 186). Charlie tells Manuel he does not even know what the word "paternalism" means, yet he confronts Danny and Old Man Ortiz on Anita's behalf. Later, when hard times make it necessary to let Lupe and the Flores family go, Charlie finds Lupe a job in San Angelo.

As time passes, Charlie changes his feelings to some degree about Mexicans, or at least "his" Mexicans. He "gradually begins to see the Mexican-Americans in his world as individuals" (*Time* 64). And he comes to realize how much he cares about them. They are not just "Mexicans." They are his friends. When Lupe and his family leave for San Angelo, Charlie is overcome. Realizing things will never be the same, "The tears were working down his own cheeks as he could see them on Lupe's, and he didn't give a damn" (*Time* 236). And Charlie surprises even himself over his feelings for Teofilo Garcia, a man who has been little more to Charlie than just another Mexican Charlie calls when it is time to shear sheep and goats. But when he discovers Teofilo is ill, "Charlie clasped his hands together and looked away, blinking rapidly at the dust which stung his eyes. He had never fully realized before that he counted Teofilo as a friend" (*Time* 350).

When Charlie and Page Mauldin have a conversation about Manuel and Kathy Mauldin, who play together, Page mutters darkly, "These kids nowadays, they can't tell one color from another. I wonder sometimes what this world's comin' to." And when Page observes that if Manuel were not a Mexican he could be anything, including doctor, lawyer, or banker, Charlie responds, "I reckon he could still be any of them things if he was of a mind to. Everybody gets his chance in this country" (*Time* 54). Still, when Manuel's pony has died and the boy expresses the intention of being a vet so he can help other animals, Charlie thinks to himself that "Manuel had no more chance than a snowball in hell" (*Time* 215). By the end of the novel, however, Charlie's paternalism has given way to grateful acceptance for Manuel's help when Charlie has lost nearly everything.

Then Manuel patronizes *him*. Danny Ortiz enters the picture once again, the same Danny Ortiz that Charlie had threatened on behalf of Manuel and the entire Flores family. Charlie thinks to make a believer of Danny once and for all, but Manuel, older and no longer willing to let Charlie fight his battles for him, commands; "You sit yourself down!" (*Time* 356). Charlie sits. Finally, he persuades banker Emmett Rodale to back Manuel's dream of vet school; when Rodale brings up the fact that Manuel is a Mexican, Charlie says only, "I don't see what difference that makes, so long as he's good" (*Time* 364). Charlie, as Kenneth Davis notes in *Updating the Literary West*, "matures into as much respect as a man of Charlie's time could have" (583).

Ironically enough, it is also Charlie who is able to overcome his prejudice against the illegals who come from Mexico, though the legal Mexican-Americans often are not. When Charlie first meets the wetbacks who ask him for work, a sick, pitiful old man and his two sons, "For a moment he felt a twinge of guilt that these people were hungry and he was not, and then a brief resentment against them for arousing that guilt" (*Time* 39). Manuel Flores dismisses them as wetbacks who are not their problem. After Charlie's horse throws him in the battle with the coyote and he is hurt and helpless, he has a moment of doubt: "He stared at the young wetback, and a tug of ancient prejudice came unbidden. For a moment he felt a stir of resentment for his dependence upon this stray Mexican" (*Time* 123). As he waits for the young Mexican, Jose Rivera, to bring help, "An old Anglo feeling took hold of him: *you never can depend on a Mexican*" (*Time* 126). But the young man does come back. Gradually, as Charlie gets to know the young man who helps him, and he comes to know his name and what a skilled craftsman he is, Charlie is able to put aside his prejudice, for the most part, although he still worries that Jose may have gotten Anita Flores pregnant. Danny Ortiz, on the other hand, despises Jose, calling him a "'damn stinking wetback'" (*Time* 182). Like his father, Danny views himself as better than the other Mexicans, whether born on the Texas side of the river or the Mexican. He thinks of his own family are "Spaniards, one of the sangre puro, above the common herd" (*Time* 189). When Old Man Ortiz dies, Danny takes up where his dad left off, loan sharking to poor Mexicans, taking advantage of those in his own culture. By the end of the story Charlie doesn't think twice about asking the illegal Mexicans into his home to eat, although

> *Twenty years ago Charlie would not have asked even Diego or Anselmo into his house to eat. The line then between Mexican and Anglo had been sharply drawn. In recent times that line had become clouded and largely erased, so that Charlie rarely thought twice about asking a Mexican in. Somewhere along the way he had unconsciously drifted into acceptance of the idea so that now he did not remember it had been any other way.* (Time 246)

The younger generation is still caught in the middle by the very system they eschew. But they do a lot to overcome the old feelings, partly by joking about the differences. When Buddy Thompson and Manuel greet one another at the dance, Buddy calls Manuel "Meskin," and Manuel says, "What do you want, *gringo?*" Both boys recognize that the "words would have sent Manuel's parents into a silent fury, or left Buddy's father red-faced and stomping. But between these two young men they meant nothing; by using them they were somehow making fun of the prejudices held by an older generation" (*Time* 146). Still, Buddy tells Manuel he has always wished Anita were not a Mexican. Buddy does, though, ask Anita to dance, defying the cultural mores that dictated "An Anglo boy's motives were automatically suspect when he began paying attention to the Mexican girls, and the girls' motives were in question if they encouraged that attention" (*Time* 148). That he does not view Manuel as an equal but instead feels responsible for him becomes clear when Buddy knocks Danny over the head at the dance, telling his friend,

"I was just tryin' to take care of you" (*Time* 155). It is clearly a new day when Manuel reports to Charlie near the end of the novel that Anita and Buddy were dating, despite Buddy's father's objections.

Kathy is never troubled by Manuel's culture or ethnicity. Manuel, on the other hand, is all too painfully aware of the differences between them. It is he, after all, who occupies an inferior niche in society. As he matures, he goes from a kid who looked to Charlie for approval and protection to a young man filled with bitterness over a system that keeps him down, a system that tells him he is not capable of fighting his own battles, but must instead rely on Charlie, or Buddy Thompson, or, God forbid, on a girl to fight for him! There is a noticeable strain between Charlie and him over the incident with Danny Ortiz, which colors Manuel's feelings toward Charlie, so much so that when Charlie has no option save letting the Flores family go, "Manuel had said nothing to him, but the message in his eyes had been plain to read: *You sold us out*" (*Time* 236).

But Manuel grows up and tells Charlie, "There were things I didn't believe . . . . I had some wrong ideas for a while. I hope you'll forgive me" (*Time* 307). Manuel works to save what little Charlie has left, at no charge, ultimately calling him "Mister" Charlie, not in some antiquated form of semi-feudalism but in respect for his mentor's age and wisdom and endurance: "Mister Charlie, don't you know you've already paid me? All those years—even when I didn't see it—you were payin' me. However long I stay here, I'm still ahead" (*Time* 339). He is, in fact, so at peace with himself and the world that when he finally has the chance to give Danny Ortiz the beating he wanted to mete out all those years ago, he is able to restrain himself and say,

> "I'm glad you came here, Danny. I'm glad I saw you
> again because now I can heal up a sore that's festered in me
> for years." He pointed at Charlie. "You see that old man over
> yonder? There was a time once I'd have killed you—or tried

to. That old man kept me from it. I hated him for it at the time. Now I'm glad he did. You weren't worth it; you're still not worth it." (Time 357–58)

Another indication of Kelton's theme of change has to do with the intrusion of the government into the lives of the characters. These West Texas ranchers are a hardy, stubborn, fiercely independent bunch, or, as the novel reveals, they used to be. They and their forbears came to this land, armed only with strong backs and a gritty determination to make a go of it. They were like Charlie's grandfather:

"He came to this country when the Comanches still carried the only deed. Granddad, he kept his powder dry and didn't look to the government to hold his hand. He went through cruel hard times when there was others takin' a pauper's oath so they could get money and food and free seed, but he never would take that oath. He come within an inch of starvin' to death, and he died a poor man. But he never owed any man a debt he didn't pay, and he never taken a thing off of the government." (Time 53)

Neither will Charlie, though many others in his county do. Yancy and Rounder Pike, for instance, elect to take all they can get. Yancy takes even more than he is allotted, reporting livestock he does not own and receiving more feed than he is entitled to. Page Mauldin also gets his fair share from the feed program. Because he is cut from the same cloth as Charlie, he feels the need to defend his actions, telling Charlie: "Everybody takes money one way or the other, directly or otherwise. The railroads get it . . . and the airlines . . . and the schoolteachers. Half the people that go around talkin' about independence and free enterprise have got their own pipeline to the government money" (*Time* 52). Realizing he has been bought by Washington for his vote, he says, "I don't believe in it either, but I take it because it's easy money and because everybody else does" (*Time* 53).

The story line makes chillingly clear that Page's way is the way that leads to death and destruction. Compared to a wounded bobcat backed into a corner, Page struggles desperately to hang on, going ever deeper into debt. Things come to a head when the government regulators, the very men who were supposed to save him, begin gunning for Page, whom they decide never needed the subsidized feed in the first place because he could have afforded to buy his own. To make matters even worse, he reveals to his old friend, Charlie Flagg, what has motivated him all these years, hate and envy. Snubbed and made to feel inferior by his ranch boss's wife when he was young, Page has spent a lifetime acquiring more land, more cattle, more possessions. Realizing what a mess his life has been, he tells Charlie "that drouth program was the biggest [mistake]. If I hadn't ever touched it . . . if I'd stayed out of it like you done . . . maybe I wouldn't be sittin' here like this today, a ruined man" (*Time* 305). Page realizes there is only one way out of his dilemma: he shoots himself.

Charlie has no interest in getting anything for free, because he knows a fundamental truth all the others seem to have forgotten — nothing is ever free. As an agricultural writer, Kelton "witnessed the futility of most federal efforts to help. The government entered the picture with good intentions but usually managed to foul things up." On one occasion the Department of Agriculture announced on Friday afternoon that a five-dollar per ton subsidy on hay would go into effect on Monday morning. When Monday arrived, however, "hay prices had advanced ten dollars, not only nullifying the subsidy but costing its recipients an extra five dollars. Those people not in the program were ten dollars poorer" (*Sandhills Boy* 206).

It is precisely this sort of logjammed bureaucracy that Charlie Flagg so grittily opposes. Throughout the course of the novel he steadfastly refuses to take any help from the government, even when doing so would lessen his drought-induced burden. When he needs a new well he drills his own, explaining to Page, "Anything I've ever done on this ranch, I've done because I thought it was worth some-thin' to me. If it's worth buildin', I'll do it myself. If it's not worth enough for me to spend my own money on it, it's not right to ex-pect somebody else to do it . . ." (*Time* 52). He refuses to plant seed when the federal regulator explains if he does they will be able to tell him if and when to harvest it. He gets himself in hot water with the other ranchers, all of whom have been his friends for over forty years, when he tells this story to the newspaper reporter about why he will continue to do for himself:

> "If you was to go out to my ranch and look around my barn, you'd find a bunch of cats. Feed barns and haystacks are bad about breedin' mice if you don't have cats to keep them thinned out. Now, if you'd go in my wife's kitchen you'd see an old pet cat curled up close to the stove. She's fat and lazy. If a mouse was to run across the kitchen floor that old cat wouldn't hardly stir a whisker. She's been fed everything she wanted. She depends on us. If we went off someday and left her she'd starve.
>
> "But out at the barn there's cats that can spot a mouse across two corrals. I never feed them. They rustle for theirselves, and they do a damn good job of it. If I was to leave they'd never miss me. All they need is a chance to operate. They may not be as fat as the old pet, but I'd say they're healthier. And they don't have to rub somebody's leg for what they get. Now, you can call me old-fashioned if you want to—lots of people do—but I'd rather be classed with them go-getters out in the barn than with that old gravy-licker in the kitchen."
> (*Time* 289)

Though he never sets out to do so, he makes the others feel guilty. Rounder Pike explains to Charlie: "We envy you for your guts, Charlie, but I reckon we resent you a little, too, for bein' stronger than the rest of us. Times past, they used to crucify the prophets" (*Time* 295).

When the drought drags on year after year, Charlie does change his behaviors in order to survive. He sells his cattle, even though he had raised them back three and four generations. With a heavy heart he tells Lupe Flores that he and his family must leave the ranch; he can no longer afford to keep and feed them. He auctions his sheep at a deep loss. He rigs a contraption for spraying blackstrap molasses on the tobosa grass the sheep will not eat, only to have them lick it off and ignore the grass. He learns to burn the thorns off prickly pear cactus, something he swore he would never do, so the livestock can eat the pulpy leaves. With a sort of grim pleasure he even develops an effective technique of making a slow, gentle pass with the flame, and then burning the remainder of the thorn on a second pass, feeling a "glow of pride for having worked it out without being told about it" (*Time* 265). As a last resort, he once again changes his behavior. Banker Emmett Rodale has suggested buying goats all along, but Charlie will have none of it. He tells Rodale, "Outside of a few Spanish goats for meat, I never owned a goat in my life and I don't ever intend to. I'm no Ayrab" (*Time* 230).

He finally gives in, discovering to his joy and disgust the goats pay not only their own way, but pay a considerable amount toward the feed bill for the sheep as well. In all his misery, though, he does not give in and accept government aid, prompting Manuel to grudgingly admit, "The whole United State government couldn't buy him" (*Time* 356).

It is once again the younger generation that provides a sliver of hope in dealing with the changes the government program has put in place. Kathy Mauldin has watched her daddy work himself to death, constantly lusting after more land, only to die in despair. She has somehow turned out, as Charlie muses, "an open and honest girl who didn't try to be something she wasn't; she led nobody down a false trail with phony affections. You accepted her as she was or let her alone. He decided she had turned out rather well, considering that she had spent years without her mother, and with a father who was always off to hell and gone" (*Time* 279). As the screws begin inexorably tightening on her father, she attempts to save him, assuring him they still have the home ranch because her deceased mother had left it to her and they can build on it. At her dad's funeral she declares, "'It's my ranch. I'll take care of it myself.' She clenched her small fists, her voice tight. 'I'll not ever let anybody *give* me anything. And no son of a bitch—*nobody*—will ever get a chance to take away what's mine. They'll never do to me what they did to my daddy!'" (*Time* 308). And keep it she does, so that she and Manuel have a place, albeit modest, on which to start their life together.

The second overarching theme of the novel, the notion of endurance, is a natural outgrowth of the first. If, indeed, change is inevitable; if, indeed, one must in some instances alter his behavior to survive, the logical question then becomes what in this world will actually last? What will stand the test of time? One answer is that the land endures. It is, in fact, such a force in the novel that it becomes a character, exerting presence and will in order to test the men and women who inhabit it. When the novel opens, the land is already beset by drought, as these ominous words reveal:

> *It crept up out of Mexico, touching first along the brackish Pecos and spreading then in all directions, a cancerous blight burning a scar upon the land . . . . Just another dry spell, men said at first . . . . Why worry? . . . It would rain this fall. It always had. But it didn't. And many a boy would become a man before the land was green again."* (*Time* xiii-xiv)

Kelton structures the novel with painstaking care, ensuring the drought is never far from the eyes of either the characters or the reader. Of the twenty chapters in the book, fully fifteen, in addition to the prologue, begin with the drought. Chapter five, for instance, begins thus: "Nothing more than an occasional teasing rainshower found Charlie Flagg's Brushy Top ranch, hardly enough to wet a man in his shirtsleeves. The sun would steal the scant moisture almost before Charlie could ride out to see how deeply it had penetrated in the pastures . . ." (*Time* 90). Chapter ten begins, "Summer was a dry disappointment. Thunderheads boiled out of nowhere, full of fury but devoid of rain, making their show and drifting away like a teasing girl" (*Time* 194).

Though it is beaten up and hung out to dry, the land nevertheless endures, due to its hardy nature, as Kelton explains in Joyce Roach's *This Place of Memory*: "To the stranger, it can be a harsh and forbidding land where summer heat sets the horizon line to wriggling like a snake, where green grass is scarce and most forms of vegetation come armed for protection with thorns that seem to jump out and stab you" (5). The land endures by being tough, and it in turn creates tough men and women who must learn to make peace with the harsh conditions if they are to survive, and, if they are really charmed, learn to love the land.

Sam "Suds" O'Barr and Emil Deutscher best illustrate this feeling for the land. O'Barr has been the beneficiary of a canny father who, in ensuring his son never has to work, has crippled him by arranging his will in such a way that his son could never sell the land. Now he lives off what he collects in land-lease payments from Charlie and other ranchers. He explains to Charlie why he must raise the contract price for the coming year by reminding him, "That old country of mine has been right good to you through the years" (*Time* 82). Charlie sees through the ruse and further knows that all the land means or will ever mean to Suds is money for beer and chasing women. In fact, he is so moronic about the careful balancing required in keeping the land healthy that he is unable to even comprehend Charlie's questions. To Charlie's query as to what will happen to the land when O'Barr has jacked up the lease price so high the only way the rancher can afford it is to put more and more sheep and cattle on it, thereby making it look like the Sahara Desert in twenty years, O'Barr's only response is, "Twenty years from now I'll be dead!" (*Time* 84). He does, however, live to see this very thing happen. He charges Charlie's son Tom such an exorbitant lease price for the land that Tom is forced to overgraze it during the drought, in essence ruining the land. When O'Barr complains to Charlie, the rancher at least has the satisfaction of telling Suds that he guessed he had lived too long! Land will never be anything other than "a commodity to be used, traded or sold" in Sam O'Barr's mind (*Time* 82).

Emil Deutscher, on the other hand, is a man born to the land. It fills him and fulfills him as nothing else will do, and the act of planting seeds, watching them grow with what is nearly a mother's anxiousness, and finally harvesting their offspring is the only life he can imagine: "Emil Deutscher derived a strong sense of pride from standing on their land, crumbling the soil through [his] fingers, smelling the new grass, feeling the ebb and flow of life in the earth as the seasons came and went" (*Time* 82).

Even Deutscher's love for the land, however, is no match for the implacability of the drought. Late in the novel we learn that Emil and his family have been forced to relocate to Fort Worth; the years of no rain have finally broken him.

But Charlie is a man who is never, ever, *ever* giving up. He may be backed up against a rock with a game leg and a bad heart, but, as Kelton illustrates through his main character, a man must just "hang and rattle." It is this impulse that allows him to sell his livestock, to "try whatever he can think of. If the first thing don't work, try the next thing. If that don't work, go on to somethin' else. Minute a man quits tryin', he's blowed up" (*Time* 208).

As the novel ends we find him nursing a broken heart, laid up with strict orders to take it easy and heal, but again, we see him trying anything and everything to save his goats. He grabs a coat and dashes into the downpour, first using the pickup to make a make a run at the goats, "racing the motor and honking the horn, hoping to give them enough momentum to keep moving after he pulled away to look for more." Next, he tries shaking an empty feed sack at another group of shivering goats, "shouting obscenities at them in English and Spanish, slapping them across the faces." With the rain coming down in sheets, he starts a fire in the pasture, hoping some of the goats will warm themselves, only to watch in horror as those at the back push the goats closest to the fire into the flames, so that "Charlie could hear the agonized cries of animals burning alive, cries that fused with the moaning of goats freezing to death" (*Time* 370–71).

The relationship Charlie and Mary Flagg share further illuminates the necessity of hanging tough, even when giving in sometimes makes more sense, and most certainly would be simpler. In the early days of their marriage, Charlie reflects that things used to be better between them. Though they had so little, "there had been a warm sense of sharing, even when there was so little to share" (*Time* 66). And when their son wonders why they keep fighting the land and drought, Charlie explains to him, "This old country'll take care of you if you just hang in there with it and fight. Hell, don't you think I been in debt before? We bought this outfit on a shoestring, me and your mother. We come within an ace of losin' it . . . two-three times. We just hung and rattled" (*Time* 261).

Their lives were further marked with a sexual love that kept them close. As Charlie thinks back on their early married life, he remembers fondly the "eager physical love that held them together like two strong and opposite magnets" (*Time* 66–67). They no longer sit on the porch of an evening, discussing the day's events, and have so little relationship remaining that

> *Charlie didn't look forward to mealtime with much anticipation. When he and Mary were alone in the big house there was a cold emptiness Charlie couldn't get used to. It was a cavernous old place with big, lonely rooms and a deadly quiet. They seemed to have little to talk about; he had wearied of discussing dry weather, and Mary had wearied of hearing about it. (Time 117)*

They are so locked into their own hurts and longings and inability to talk with their mate about subjects mundane or weighty that they live in the sort of misery that Larry McMurtry has called the "domestic tragedy" (Pilkington 376). And while once they found pleasure in the other's body, now they sleep in separate bedrooms, each afraid to go to the other for fear of being rejected or made to feel a fool.

While perhaps most other couples would give it up and refuse to go on in this kind of mute misery, Charlie and Mary Flagg stay together, we gather, because they stood in front of a preacher and said they would. And not surprisingly, it is when life becomes truly arduous that they find their way back to one another.

Kelton employs the ongoing struggle over Charlie's weight to indicate the rift and subsequent healing in their relationship. While she offers homemade cakes, chili beans, fried potatoes, and apple pies to others, Mary bypasses Charlie and instead plops turnip greens on his plate. She gives the Mexicans leftover pie rather than saving it for Charlie and never misses a chance to "spoon out another helping of greens for Charlie and tell him in the presence of all that he needed to lose some weight" (*Time* 248). Mary first begins softening toward Charlie when he has stood up to the entire bunch of his friends, refusing to go to Washington on their behalf, hanging tough for what he believes in, doing for himself or doing without. When Tom has dogged him for not going along with the others, he turns to Mary, expecting her to chew him out as well. Instead, she says, "There's still a slice of that chocolate cake left. You want it?" (*Time* 257). Finally, as she watches Charlie worry and work himself into a heart attack, it is she who is now pushing her husband to eat when he would rather be standing in the yard searching for the rain that never comes. Her cooking, which she has withheld from him, just as she has withheld her love, she now offers freely.

Their emotional and sexual healing begins with that most basic of human impulses, a touch. As Charlie weeps unashamedly when the Flores family leaves the ranch for good, expecting Mary to chide him for refusing the government aid that would have allowed him to keep the hired help, he is surprised when she instead "slipped her hand into his and leaned against him in a way she hadn't done for years" (*Time* 237). And when Tom once again goads his father about the elder Flagg's refusal to sacrifice his principles and become bedfellows with the government, Mary defends her husband, telling the boy, "Son, when a man believes in a thing strongly enough, there *is* a price too high to pay. There is a point where compromise costs him too much" (*Time* 271). Returning to their first love allows the couple to pull together once again, as they used to do.

They also find sexual contentment, the final component in their restoration as a couple, when Mary, instead of waiting for Charlie to come to her bed, goes to his instead: "Mary felt for the covers and crawled in beside him. It surprised him; he couldn't remember *when* she had ever come to his bed . . . . She kissed him on the forehead. He lay a moment, wondering, then he reached for her as he used to do a long time ago" (*Time* 283). They have come such a long way, in fact, that they can meet the future together, confident of their love for one another and as sure as ever of the values they share, values Ira Blanton identifies in his Kelton dissertation as "a tenacious insistence on self-reliance and the necessity and dividends of hard work" (136). And it is literally together we see them at the end of the novel, walking back to the house: "He laid his heavy arm around Mary's shoulder. 'I think me and you need some hot coffee. Come on, woman, let's go to the house'" (*Time* 373).

The final value played out in the novel is the importance of leaving the world a better place than it was when we got here. Charlie takes this cultural injunction seriously, and does the best he knows how to do with the land, intent on leaving it in good condition for Tom and those who follow along behind. If they have used the land unwisely, as Charlie says, it is not because they have a desire to be profligate with the land, but only that they do not know any better.

Besides caring for the land, the other way these characters' lives improve the world is by passing on their values to the next generation. Kathy Mauldin, Manuel Flores, and, most important, Tom Flagg illustrate just how much the values their parents and others have done their best to impart have actually taken hold. Kathy has become nearly as passionate about taking help from anyone as Charlie, after watching it destroy her father. Declaring her intention of never giving up the fight against the drought, she informs Charlie when he suggests she consider leasing the land to others, "No, this is my place, and it'll *stay* my place. Nobody's goin' to beat me out of what's mine . . . not any calculatin' banker, not any short-weightin' cow buyer, not any starch-shirted government man with a satchel full of papers. I'm stayin' right here'" (*Time* 347).

Manuel demonstrates his own tenacity when he returns to the ranch to help Charlie save it, working free of charge. When the rains come, he understands the danger it poses to the goats. Charlie is on his way out to rescue them when Mary tells him it is too risky for his newly damaged heart, and she will wake Manuel. She does not have a chance, though, because "Manuel was only a few steps behind him, fumbling with a slicker" (*Time* 366). In conditions that would have made most return to the house and give up on the goats, Manuel gets on a horse, in the driving rain, with lightning flashing all about him, and does his best to turn the goats toward the barn, all the while expressing concern for "Mister Charlie." As their efforts fail, in spite of doing all they can, Charlie finally realizes it is too late, but "Manuel was sobbing, still carrying on the struggle, his tears washed away by the rain that pelted his face" (*Time* 372). He takes Charlie's burdens as his own, so much so that Charlie tells Emmett Rodale he has raised *two* good boys, Manuel and Tom.

It is, finally, Tom who provides the best example of benchmarks worth keeping being passed down to the next generation. At first glance, and indeed, through much of the novel, he comes across as a selfish, cocksure young man who gives not one whit about the things that matter most to his father. And, like every parent, Charlie wonders if anything he has tried to teach the boy has stuck. When we first meet Tom he is twenty-two, the perfect image of the arrogant cowboy, even though many times Lupe Flores has had to pull him "out of a jackpot so easily that Tom never realized he had even been in trouble" (*Time* 19). He is in love with the rodeo, and over and over again, just when Charlie needs him the most, he hightails it back to the rodeo circuit, convinced he is going to win big. Even when things have gone from bad to worse with Charlie, as year after year he struggles to make do with no rain, Tom still refuses to leave the rodeo life to help his father. Granted, the flashy rodeo groupie he has married will not allow it if he does want to leave, but he never even makes the effort. When an injury forces him back to the ranch, he helps out only because he has no other options. And even then his interior life is still filled with dreams of winning big dollars, some of which he promises Charlie he will send home. Charlie knows better; Tom has never sent a dime home, even when he was making a respectable living riding and roping. Things come to a head when he loses patience with his dad's refusal to accept government intervention: "You're livin' in the past. Drive by the employment commission office sometime and look at all them lazy sons of bitches lined up for relief checks when there's people tryin' to hire them for honest work. You think they worry about somebody else helpin' pay their bills?" (*Time* 268). He is so sure that his dad is wrong that he insists on dividing up the livestock and property; he will keep the O'Barr leased land and Charlie will keep the other leased land and his own deeded land. It is with a heavy heart that Charlie then watches his son get himself ever deeper in debt, doubting anything he has tried so hard to get across has sunk into his son's wayward head: "I oughtn't to've waited so long to talk things out with you. I ought to've talked to you more when you was a boy, so you'd of come up thinkin' right" (*Time* 270).

When Big Emmett Rodale looks to chew Charlie's hide for his son's latest irresponsibility, Charlie has to hear the news from the banker:

> *"Well, he's gone, Charlie. Best I can tell, they packed up what stuff was in the house and shipped it to his wife's home in Dallas. He loaded that girl into the car and that ropin' horse into the trailer, and he took off to find him a rodeo. He gave me a phone call as he was gassin' up at the fillin' station; said he was checkin' it to me and the FHA to wrestle it out between us the best way we could." (Time 281)*

With a heavy heart Charlie must come to terms with the fact that his son is a quitter, that when he most needs him, Tom lights a shuck and runs away. He has seemingly deserted the principles Charlie has tried so valiantly to make sure his son absorbs, to say nothing of a mountain of debt and land he has ruined by so over-grazing that it may never recover. He is forced to admit, "I thought I'd taught him everything I knew. I taught him how to ride and rope and judge stock. I taught him how to gauge his grass in the fall and how to bring an animal through a hard winter. But I forgot to teach him the way I think. Now it's too late for him to learn" *(Time 274)*.

Charlie Flagg is wrong about this, though. Yes, his son is immature and arrogant, as young men are prone to be. Yes, he has made some regrettable decisions, not the least of which is marrying Dolly Ellender, who divorces him for some other hotshot rodeo star when Tom is sidelined, but in the things that matter, Tom does share his father's values, and is almost comically like Charlie in ways small and large. When Charlie's friends all order boggy-top pie [pie with no top crust] at the café, Charlie, just to be contrary, orders doughnuts. When the rodeo organizers ask Tom to park in a certain spot outside the arena, he instead maneuvers his truck right into the middle of the lot they are trying to keep clear. Like his dad, Tom refuses to listen to the doctor's advice, cutting the cast off his leg himself when Doc Fancher will not because the leg is not healed properly.

Tom Flagg, though, demonstrates his ability to hang and rattle, just like his old dad. The banker Emmett Rodale drives out to Brushy Top ranch to tell Charlie about it: "He's been havin' pretty good luck on the rodeo circuit, and he got some money ahead. He sent me a check. Said he'd do it again as soon as he could, and keep on doin' it till he got his debt squared off." He tells the stunned Charlie, "All them lessons you taught him, they took better than you thought they did . . . . Goes to show that a man shouldn't lose faith in his young just because they dance to a different music. They'll do the right thing in the end, most of them, if they've been brought up the proper way" (*Time* 362). The lessons, Charlie realizes, have stuck.

As the novel ends, the rain begins. That is not to say, however, that all is well. In fact, at first glance it would appear that little hope remains for the major characters, especially Charlie Flagg. True, the rain signals the end of the drought, but the story does not end there. Kelton novels generally do not provide a uniformly cheery ending, and he explains why:

> I have taken a lot of abuse for the final chapter of that book. It seems most readers would rather have had the story wrap up with a good rain, and everybody happy. But life isn't often that generous. The rest of the book was patterned after life, and I thought it would be a betrayal to have it end with all the loose ends tied up neatly and all problems solved. (*Living* 20)

Charlie has lost nearly everything by this time. The cattle have been sold. The sheep have been sold. He has been forced to subsist on his own deeded property, rather than operating on the ten thousand acres to which he is accustomed. The land is so scorched and starved that its recovery will likely take several more years, all of which has led critics to conclude that all is lost, or very nearly so, for Charlie: "At novel's end there appears little hope for a new beginning—at least not for Charlie. He is too old and too debilitated" (Pilkington 376).

The novel's conclusion, however, is lush with hope, even in the face of overwhelmingly dreary odds. Hope emerges in the young. Kathy Mauldin and Manuel Flores come and fight the good fight with Charlie and Mary, working to save a few more goats even when Charlie and Mary have given up and gone home. They are so invested with the values passed down to them that any other behavior is unthinkable. And even though the land is frail and damaged, it, too offers hope, as Charlie realizes: "There's still the land . . . . A man can always start again. A *man* always *has* to" (*Time* 373). Finally, Charlie has lost many of his material possessions, but he has found his way back to something far more valuable, and that is the true partnership he shares with Mary, symbolized when he defies her by going out to save the goats. He tells his wife, "I'm not stayin' here, woman. Them's my goats." She swiftly corrects him by saying, "*Our* goats" (*Time* 366). He has rediscovered what has been there all along—a woman who stands by him, who believes in him, who is willing to help him with and through anything that comes their way. As they listen to the dying cries of most of their goats, he looks to her for strength: "He saw little hope there now, but he remembered other times when there had been little hope. He knew how it would be. Today those blue eyes would cry. Tomorrow the life would start showing again, and they would begin to hope, to calculate, to plan" (*Time* 373). It is clear that she is now his anchor, and so they can walk together, shoulder-to-shoulder, to meet a new day.

Heroic men like Charlie, who possess the same kind of pioneering spirit of their grandfathers before them, who defy the odds, who are willing to stand alone to defend their beliefs, are buoyed by the knowledge that "their values will endure, and it is the land, the women, and the young generations who teach them that lesson" (Blanton 130–31). That Kelton reminds us all of such truths with eminently believable characters and carefully constructed plot lines marks him as not just a fine genre writer, but rather a "great American novelist—no 'Western' modifier necessary" (http://www.frontporchrepublic.com/2009/08/elmer-kelton-rip/).

Convergence: Race and Ethnicity in the Work of Elmer Kelton

Joyce Roach

A LINE OF VERSE BY Townsend Miller in *This Bitterly Beautiful Land* suggests the theme that runs through the novels of Elmer Kelton. Miller calls the region of Kelton's works, "The bleached bone laid on the huge heart of the continent." The 1972 book, edited by Al Lowman, the great Texas bibliophile, contains essays, recollections, and descriptions of a land that is indeed bitterly beautiful. Long out of print, the book is a limited edition designed by William Holman, illustrated by Barbara Whitehead, and published by Roger Beacham. Though it does not directly discuss the works of Elmer Kelton, it paints a picture of the land he loved and wrote about. What he calls in his memoir *Sandhills Boy*, his *Heimat*, his homeland.

The title of Lowman's book could serve as an epigraph for all the works of Elmer Kelton, for he is concerned with characters, often racially and culturally dissimilar, who make habitable the inhospitable in an impossible climate and a forbidding landscape. Juxtaposing the bitter and beautiful is always present, but so is balancing the two.

Most critics maintain, arguably, that the focal point of many of Kelton's stories is cowboy/ranching life, but add that race, culture, socio-economic status, gender, history, and folklore attached to every group within the arid stretches of the Southwest in general and West Texas in particular validate the story and illustrate his personal vision. There is collision and cohesion in all these elements; conflict and resolution; difference and likeness; consequences and changes; mixing or separating. In other words, convergence, wherein all notions meet.

Nothing means more than location, a coming together of a multitude of Southwestern components in a specific region of the American Southwest, with West Texas as dead center for the novelist. But even dead center covers thousands of square miles and millions of acres, not to mention some 500 years of history, recorded and unrecorded.

Both the Southern Plains and the Chihuahuan Desert, two geographic regions, converge too. Both regions are, or were, largely uninhabitable, or at the very least inhospitable and populated with indigenous peoples (Comanches mainly), transplanted inhabitants (Mexicans mainly), invasive conquerors (early Spanish, but later Anglo settlers, mainly), or those passing through (cavalry, trail-drivers)—all of whom have notable cultural and racial differences, both intra- as well as inter-group.

THE PLACE OF CONVERGENCE . . .

The *place* of convergence means everything—shapes, molds, changes, destroys, makes noble and ignoble individuals. Place also impacts ethnicity—the ways (habits, customs, speech, living, thinking, adapting) and means of a racial or cultural group.

Geographic determinism comes into play here: how the regions of the earth shape the animal kingdom, mankind included, and contribute to who and what they are and how they behave. J. Frank Dobie used the phrase, "appropriate to time and place," referring to the behavior of people in Old-Time Texas.

In *Elmer Kelton and West Texas* (1988), Judy Alter writes:

> *The always accurate but fairly casual mention of the land's characteristics in the early works is replaced in later*

works, particularly the major novels, by an almost lyrical un-
derstanding of West Texas, its harsh nature and its under-
appreciated beauty, and of the men who have peopled that
land. The rugged harshness and beauty of the West are not
just thematic; they are also contributing factors in the devel-
opment of Kelton's characters. (127)

Kelton acknowledges his part of Texas, harsh as it is, marks, defines, integrates, and anchors real people and therefore his characters with a sense of place, of belonging, becoming a part of. He
notes that the Mexican people call such a feeling *querencia* (Kelton, "What's Wrong in Being Different?" 9).

In a preface to *Texian Stompin' Grounds*, a 1941 volume of the
Texas Folklore Society, Harry Ransom put it this way:

Among the feelings that have moved men powerfully,
none has been more universal than love of the earth. Con-
sciously or unconsciously, silently or in defiant proclama-
tions, men have always identified themselves with their na-
tive soil. With their own countryside, with their home rock,
they have associated the forces of their lives. Young men,
not always in vain, have died for this ideal of the land; po-
ets have sung it and old men have celebrated it in story. It
has made some men narrow, but it has made others heroic.
Famed or nameless, each of us is moved by this feeling for
the place of his growth. Every man deserves a native heath."
(xvii)

The work of Elmer Kelton affirms Ransom's declaration. Lyrical, soft, affectionate allusions to the land of West Texas are often
just that and belie or underplay the realities of it. It is often through
the personalities of his characters who must struggle, live or die with
it, that attest to the realities of Place.

The main character in *Stand Proud* who speaks to this feeling is

Frank Claymore, a "strong-willed, individualistic breed," one "whose years of struggle had etched a belligerent independence into his grain," even a violent streak, who "never called on others for help, not even from God" (2–7). In spite of a personality forged in hard times in hard environment, Claymore's relationship with the land draws him, speaks to him, inspires his devotion, but it is a woman who finally helps him make peace with himself. Still, Letty is linked to Claymore's feelings about the ranch in unspoken ways, albeit the place that forged Claymore's abrasive personality.

The same kind of negative aspects in character infect Wes Hendrix (*The Man Who Rode Midnight*) as he fights to keep his home and land from becoming a lake. His reasoning is that he doesn't live in just a house; he "lives everywhere his land is" (110). In the afterword to the novel, Kenneth Davis, a West Texan himself, insists that people draw strength from the harsh, raw environment where to survive at all is nearly impossible. Not a few of Kelton's characters become like the land — stubborn, mean- spirited, fractious, hateful.

While the land may be a catalyst for the behavior of Frank and Wes, citing only two of Kelton's novels, the land does not make its presence felt beyond descriptions, or casual mention, as Alter notes. However, in the later novels such as *The Time it Never Rained, The Wolf and the Buffalo*, and *Honor at Daybreak*, Place is a major character, making itself known in its extremes of weather. It is in such works that the locale of convergence is painfully noticeable. Lyrical description of such places are few. Realistic description takes precedence.

Not until *Sandhills Boy: The Winding Trail of a Texas Writer* (2007) did Kelton describe in his own words, not just through short passages of brief description, or in the dialogue of his characters, the place written mostly about — West Texas or lands like it:

> *No stranger seeing the land for the first time would describe it as scenic. It is like the ugly child loved only by its*

mother. For centuries after venturesome Spaniards first set foot there, travelers pushed across the dry stretches of West Texas on their way somewhere else. Few saw anything that invited them to stay. Water was scarce, grass was sparse. Most forms of flora and fauna were armed with stickers, thorns, horns, or tusks. Roads were few and distances long. Each seemingly barren horizon, when reached, yielded to another much the same. Prolonged droughts were the rule, punctuated by occasional times of healing rains that never seemed to heal quite enough before the next siege of dry years. It was the last part of the state to be settled, and then only because nothing else was left. (12)

There is nothing more graphic or painful to read wherein the vicious vagaries of weather and landscape and the entanglement—another word that speaks to convergence—occur than *The Time It Never Rained* (1973). The reader is choked and consumed with sun, heat, and sand only to drown in rains that come much too late.

In the Prologue to the story, Kelton sets the stage:

It crept up out of Mexico, touching first along the brackish Pecos and spreading then in all directions, a cancerous blight burning a scar upon the land.

Just another dry spell, men said at first. Ranchers watched waterholes recede to brown puddles of mud that their livestock would not touch. They watched the rank weeds shrivel as the west wind relentlessly sought them out and smothered them with its hot breath. They watched the grass slowly lose its green, then curl and fire up like dying cornstalks.

Men grumbled, but learned to live with the dry spells if you stayed in West Texas; there were more dry spells than wet ones. No one expected another drought like that of '33. And the really big dries like 1918 that came once in a lifetime.

Why worry? they said. It would rain this fall. It always had. But it didn't. And many a boy would become a man before the land was green again. (xiv)

Taking place in the Drought of the 1950s, a time remembered in agricultural histories in capital letters, what begins with Charlie Flagg's battle with malicious elements turns into a fight with friends, neighbors, the bank, his son, and the federal government. The realities of grappling with the West Texas land itself without drought are made known throughout the novel, but Charlie's attachment and fondness for the rugged, hard landscape doesn't really come under a microscope until drought attacks with a vengeance. While others give in and quit fighting a losing battle, Charlie never does. He manages to separate the forces of nature from the place itself because the land is embedded in him, the cause of his joy as well as his sorrow, the very reason for his being. As such he is determined to maintain his stubborn independence, his rugged individualism. He thinks he does not need anybody to help him. The elements are chancy and unpredictable; so is life for those who live there. A man accepts and struggles with it in order to stay on the land he constantly fights nature for. It doesn't make much sense; in fact, no sense at all—that is unless Kelton's writing sorts it out, causing readers to shake their heads, but getting it in the end. Charlie is convinced that the past and the way things used to be are his anchor, but the truth is that the land is his succor.

The time-worn adage of taking care of the land so it will take care of you is hollow, romantic nonsense. Still, Charlie and the land endure together, but only in that sense do they take care of each other:

"Outlasting this eternal drouth had become the only thing that mattered any more to Charlie. All else faded from importance; it was a vendetta" (265). For Charlie "the drouth was the beginning, the middle, and the end of his conscious thoughts" (266).

Man, beast, the earth itself, suffer and die. Drought pervades, drives the action and reaction of characters great and small who march to the rhythm of a searing, sun-pulsed beat. No lyrical descriptions here.

In *The Wolf and the Buffalo*, the same water-starved land becomes a Who, a character, in the novel that recalls the Battle of Adobe Walls of 1874 in which, historically, Comanches attacked the trading post, defeating a significant number of a cavalry unit. In Kelton's hands history becomes a dry-drama in which the Comanche draw a cavalry, composed mostly of Buffalo Soldiers, into the waterless wastes to a place appropriately called Dry Lake. From a distance the Indians take in the scene of soldiers, delirious, hallucinating, dying of thirst. One Comanche remarks: "It is the land that kills them, not us" (348).

If *Honor at Daybreak* seems an unlikely novel as illustration of West Texas characteristics, it bears notice since it takes place at a later time than Kelton usually sets his stories. If the coming of settlers, ranchers, developers, cavalry is looked on as the first harvest, the oil-patch days may be looked on as a second harvest—ravaging the same land for entirely new purposes of gleaning the leftovers, forcing not only water, but oil from the impenetrable, stubborn soil.

The landscape becomes littered with new shapes and heights forged out of man-made materials that can be as dangerous as anything rough, jagged, sharp, and treacherous in the natural landscape and terrain. Still, it is the same old sandy, rocky, windy place but in the Roaring Twenties, a period when there is little to no movement within the Place and life is settled. The story occurs at the end of the American Dream and death of the cattle kingdoms. Caprock, the fictional name of the town that resembles Kelton's Crane, is dull, finished, and living with the aftermath of the Frontier Myth. Manifest Destiny, however—that philosophy alive and well even today, often called Entrepreneurship and Big Business—causes the town to come alive when oil erupts, literally blowing holes in the earth.

Not only does the land reverberate with noisy oilfield equipment, but new and noisy cars and motorcycles that tear up the land with ruts and trails. The town is littered with the temporary—tents communities, box-houses that can be carted on wagons to other sites, sheet-iron shacks, oil rigs and ancillary equipment. No one intends to stay. The Place isn't worth anything. The junk will either be transported to other rigs or left where it is, littering the land forever. Of course, a few of the old-time residents know that's no way to treat the land, yet most are glad to take the money from leasing and drilling.

Honor at Daybreak received mixed reviews and does not stand among readers' favorites. Yet, it is still a realistic story about the arid stretches of nothing of West Texas. The land is not a character, does not drive the action, or even influence it except indirect stubbornness to yield its treasures, but man figured out a way to do even that. Thus, the worthless, wasted region provides a realistic setting.

THOSE WHO CONVERGED . . .

Identifying who all met in the Place, seems a snap even to a casual reader of Kelton's novels—cowboys, ranchers, Indians, Mexicans, and eventually cavalry, including blacks in the form of Buffalo Soldiers, a few Germans.

Some of Kelton's earlier works identify ethnic groups in Texas and the conflicts that result. In *Eyes of the Hawk* (1998), Thomas Canfield takes notice that "Texas wasn't just leftover Mexicans and Bible-speaking, whisky drinking, rifle-shooting, English-speaking immigrants from Tennessee" but "people from all over the world because it was so big and had much land to offer. You found settlements of Germans, Swedes, Irish, French, Czechs. It was Babel without a tower. It was a melting pot that never quite melted" (9).

While the mixtures of folk are indeed converging on Texas, what amounts to a listing is merely that. The story isn't about immigrants converging on Texas. It is rather about the good and bad Americans with their big wagons and the good and bad Mexicans with their big ox-carts. The two groups collide.

Canfield, who speaks Spanish and depends on Amadore to be

in charge of Mexican carters, notes "Some Mexicans will lie to you, cheat you, kill you. But some whites will do the same. What's the difference?" (9). It is the land that offers both groups the same challenges.

Bitter Trail (1997) mixes the good/bad of Anglo and Mexican, but in a slightly different way. Two characters have borrowed accoutrements, even names, from each other's culture, producing a hybrid found in other of Kelton's early works. Frio Wheeler, an Anglo with a Spanish first name, wearing a flat brimmed black American hat asks a question of "Sombreroed Blas Talamantes." Blas turns "in his big horned Mexican saddle" (1). Frio touches his "big-rowled Mexican spurs to his sorrel's ribs" (1) His skin "was burned Mexican-brown from sun" in his blue eyes (1). Blas Talamentes wears Mexican "leather breeches decorated with lacing" (1). They have borrowed until it's hard to tell them apart. "Wheeler was *patron* and Talamente was the man hired. But they were *compadres* though hard to tell *patron* from *empleado*"(2). What they wear and the equipment they use has to do with adapting to the conditions of Place—sun, heat, stickers, rocks, sand. Even their work relationship is blurred because it takes what each knows about the land to keep them both alive; a partnership to combat both the place and the gang stealing Frio's carts and mules. Who? Florencio Chapa and his *bandidos, muy malo,* composed partly of Gringos, one of whom used to be Frio's best friend. Both groups already know how to cope with the land, but it is still a region where both contend for right-of-way.

While the earlier novels take notice of the land and its effects on characters, it is in the later novels wherein the "bitterly beautiful land" marks many of the characters. *The Wolf and the Buffalo* is the premier example of race and ethnicity—Mexican, black, Anglo, Comanche, cavalry, horse culture, slave culture, newcomer, ancient dwellers, women—who converge on the rugged Southern Plains.

The work contains not one story but two, as Lawrence Clayton explains in an Afterword to the 1986 reprint by TCU Press:

In a sense, The Wolf and the Buffalo *is two novels skillfully interwoven to create a sympathetic picture of two quite
different cultures locked in a fight to the death. One of these
stories follows a young Negro, Gideon Ledbetter, out of slav-
ery in Louisiana after the Civil War ends and into the role of
a black cavalryman, one of those the Indians called buffalo
soldiers because their black curly hair resembled the shaggy
bison or buffalo. Ledbetter serves most of his time in the Tenth
U.S. Cavalry stationed at Fort Concho, located in present-
day San Angelo. Through him, Kelton depicts the plight of a
freed but still socially inferior man with the drive and ability
to succeed when given a chance; the cavalry gives him that
chance. (422)*

The second story centers on Gray Horse, a Comanche whose
tribes still rule the Southern Plains during the time when Gideon
appears. It is Gray Horse who takes center stage in the first chapter
as he seeks a vision for his life that will allow him to go into battle for
his people; in essence, to become a man. The totem, a wolf, appears
as his guide and he receives a spiritual connection to the animal.
Other images appear and become tangled in the foretelling of his
future in ways he cannot understand but make themselves clear as
the story unfolds.

To the Plains Indians, certain landscapes are sacred. Such is the
case for Gray Horse when he goes to the place called the Double
Mountains to seek his vision that will guide his life. He knows "the
spirits would surely seek out the high points" (4).

The word, mountains, calls to mind greener, cooler climes, but
such is not the case in West Texas. The rugged steeps are covered in
gravel, rocks, boulders, low growing brush, and prickly pear. Adept
as Gray Horse is in coping with rough country, he injures himself
seriously when he loses his footing:

"Gray Horse was almost to the top when the loose gravel slipped
beneath his moccasins. He slid on his stomach, moving faster as

he went down. The sharp rocks gouged and ripped at him. . . . He slammed his left leg against a boulder and stopped" (7). After inching his way to a "small patch of short, dry grass" he pulled "it up by handfuls," "wadded it tightly and pressed it against the wound," stopping the bleeding (7).

Against all odds, the questing man makes it to the top of the treacherous incline where a "warm wind, almost hot" and typical of wind conditions in such places, blows against his wound, causing healing to begin.

Later, he comes upon prickly pear cactus:

> *Gingerly, avoiding the bigger thorns, he cut away several of the pear pads, impaled them on a stick and carried them back to his waiting place on the rimrock. Using a sharp-edged flint knife, he sliced a pad open, laid it across the gash as a poultice and tied it in place with a soft leather string. Though he had cut away the large thorns, his fingertips were pierced by the tiny ones, most no larger than a human hair but wickedly sharp and persistent. Some unkind spirit had armed the prickly pear with many weapons for self-defense, as it had done with the mesquite and many forms of brush, and the other kinds of cactus. All these plants were useful, but all extracted a payment. The tiny thorns would bedevil him for days, taking their small revenge. (12–13)*

It is in the place of the Double Mountains that Gray Horse receives the wolf-medicine from dreams, visions, signs, and images brought on by extreme hunger and thirst that cause hallucination. It is the land that both critically injures him but also restores him because he knows how to listen and see into the sacred places as well as to make use of the land to sustain and heal himself—the same kinds of conditions that Gideon Ledbetter faces with far different results.

Others, such as the Texas Rangers or the Comancheros, neither of whom are intimidated by either the land or the Comanche, were "always transient, always strangers in an inhospitable land that rejected them quickly" (167). Grey Horse is confident the Buffalo Soldiers fall into the same category.

Gideon Ledbetter and even Jimbo enter the military as blank slates waiting to be written on. Coming from the southern slave culture where they are used to being told what to do and never asked to think for themselves, they also come from an entirely different kind of ecology and land mass. Accustomed to the vertical perspective of looking up and down because they are surrounded by trees, forests, thick understory providing shade and the comforts of forests—reliable water sources, wood for fires and building shelter, domesticated animals for food such as pigs, chickens, milk cows, but not necessarily beef—the woods confine perspective. Living on a plantation surrounded by the boundaries of that culture yet never partaking except for taking orders, Gideon and Jimbo are tools.

Both enter the world of horizontal perspectives—the Plains, where the only constant is space. And a good part of the story notices Gideon's trouble with it. Taken apart from the plot and action of the story, the effects of the solitary land make a personal story in itself and mark the changes in Gideon from being completely unsure of himself in such an environment to complete confidence in commanding himself and others.

As it turns out, Jimbo has little trouble adapting to cavalry life because he has been a groom for the master; he is a master of horses. He "spoke two languages, English and horse." In his position, if one can call it that, Jimbo was able to think for himself and make decisions and his judgment was reliable and trusted when it came to horseflesh.

Horses and the horse culture were central to both Indian life and cavalry life. They were beasts of burden and means of transportation; carried warriors and military into battle; accepted as barter and for buying things such as wives, or given as gifts by the Plains Indians. Or used as shields to fight behind or for eating if necessity arose.

Gideon has neither Jimbo's experience nor the Comanche

life-way to cope with the distance and space that surrounds him. Gideon never comes to complete comfort in the saddle, but it affords him confidence in a way he never quite acknowledges: Several passages allude to his maturing opinion about the country, his admiration of it, yet no mention is made except casually about his horse: "The immensity of this country, the most incomprehensible distances, seemed overpowering to him, fearsome yet strangely exhilarating"(50); yet he is terrified that Indians are watching him, hidden in all that space and ready to attack. It is the space more than human presence that assaults him.

Later in the story when Gideon comes across two dead soldiers who have met their fate because of stupid mistakes, he is sickened yet feels "that unaccountable soaring of spirit when he had faced his enemies. He would always respect this country and its dangers, but he would never be afraid of it again. He stood up to its challenge, and he had prevailed" (115).

On patrol and out of the safety of the fort, Gideon responds to his present state of affairs:

> *Every hill he climbed spread a fresh and different scene before him. It was not a planned and ordered land, with houses and fields and well-defined roads, but a new and unspoiled country with a random scattering of creeks and rivers, of mountains and prairies violated by only a few twin-rut military roads hard to distinguish from the buffalo trails that led to water, when there was any.* (130)
>
> *Sometimes Gideon had the feeling that he had set foot there the day after God had finished it, for man had made little mark upon it. The Indian neither built nor tore down, and the whiteman, for the most part, had not yet claimed it.* (131) ·

His fear for this big open land had left him. But the awe remained (131).

On the same journey, the unit passes the last water and moves into even more impressive landscape.

> *The semi-arid flatlands which sloped gradually westward toward the Pecos River, are harsh and inhospitable. Grass was sparse, and trees did not grow at all, except for a scattering of the indomitable mesquite. . . . Great open flats were covered by low shrubs like the lotebush and the greasewood, and on harder ground, up the sides of arid stony hills, grew a wicked-looking cactus plant whose curled leaves grew in a circular pattern with the sharpness and toughness of short, bent swords called "lechugilla." (131)*

Lieutenant Hollander pauses with a sense of excitement as he is able to mark a waterhole not on the map. At this point that Gideon recognizes the feeling Gray Horse, whom he has never encountered except in battle, has always been aware of:

> *A chill played on Gideon's spine as he realized they had moved onto that mysterious land known as "the plains." Men talked of it in the same mystic tones they applied to heaven and hell. The horizon line appeared level, without a tree, a hill, anything to break the flatness of it. Up there, somewhere beyond the shimmering heat waves, lay some dark and hidden stronghold known only to Comanche and Kiowa. Few white men had done more than guess at what it was like, for nature guarded it even more fiercely than the Indian. (134)*

Later, when the troops return to town, Gideon's transformation is complete:

> *Small as it was, that town frightened him more than the half-explored Indian lands that stretched almost to infinity beyond it. He had tasted that land now. For all its strange-*

*ness, its continuous threat of disaster, it produced a stimula-
tion he had never known before. Out there he seemed set free
from the constraints of his blackness. The land made equal
demands upon all men and neither gave credit nor demanded
extra for their color. (145)*

It is just as Gideon begins his ascent into a full understanding
of his potential and power in what amounts to a new world for him,
Gray Horse rapidly descends from the very same place that lets him
down, destroys his medicine, shows all his visions, dreams, of buffalo, a red calf, and wolf to be revealed as signs of his own and his
people's destruction. He recognizes that "Visions were seldom exactly like life. And life was almost never like the visions" (401).

Just before his death, Gray Horse returns to the place, the Double Mountains, where his manhood began, to the place "he could
see this great land in one long, sweeping glance that reminded him
forcefully how much the People had truly lost" (406).

Only when the setting is fully defined and the characters' places
in that setting clearly established does the novel move into more action, plot, denouement, and conclusion. Skirmishes, rescue, the last
combat with desert and thirst, death of cavalry black and white, their
mounts, the disintegration of Gray Horse's band, death of his son,
and betrayal of his totems takes precedence over Place.

Certainly examples of convergence of Buffalo Soldier and Comanche are pronounced in the novel, but others are present, too.
Different varieties of women appear at Fort Concho or in town.
Mexican women are merely used as prostitutes and never appear
in traditional roles. In fact, Mexicans play no part in the story beyond servicing the needs of soldiers, or as sources for Comanche
raids into Mexico. None are even given names. Hannah York is a
slave to Granny, also black, who farms her out both as a prostitute
and housekeeper for Elizabeth Thomas. Hannah engages in a star-
crossed love affair with Gideon. Elizabeth, wife of the commander
of the post, "tries diligently to present a symbol of polite civilization

as she remembered or imagined that civilization to be. She was an island of gentility in a huge, rough wilderness, a tiny candle in a dark night, a reminder to those who saw her that somewhere life was—or had been—different" (73). Such a description indicates Elizabeth's response to this isolated military post in the middle of a desert wilderness with all its hardships.

There is Adeline Rutledge, sister of a soldier, who comes to visit the post, and sets her cap for Lieutenant Hollander, who has been rejected earlier by a woman because he commands a black unit in the wastelands of the west. Adeline is already schooled in military life and not subject to dictates of Victorian female notions. In fact, none of the females in Kelton's story have any problems with life on the plains primarily because they are schooled as military wives and sweethearts or were prairie- and plains-born such as Green Willow. The few who might have proved examples of convergence stayed home.

There is always the feeling that people of drought-driven plains and desert, whether born there or converging there, are superior, better to know because they have scraped up against such hard country, been shaped and disciplined by it and endure. Kelton takes some pride, it seems to me, in illustrating what happens to some characters and how they are perceived when taken out of their natural element; or better yet, when they come into the region because of circumstances of choice or chance. Consider Gideon Ledbetter and Jimbo, who come not only from the South but from a slave culture; Victor Underwood (*Honor at Daybreak*), accused of being a college professor who comes to the oil fields to wildcat; or Big Boy Daugherty from East Texas who aims to kill; or Irish who had spent his childhood in East Dallas. These are only a few examples of many. Sometimes, within the racial depictions, Kelton explores the types within a race, socio-economic distinctions and levels, values, customs, ways of living—all different in their likenesses. Then he lets that mixture touch, come together, collide, change, adapt—or not.

Kelton makes the case that the land, the place he writes about inspires contentiousness, causing us to notice that the harder, more deprived the land, the more contentious some become. It is a land with so much space that people feel compelled to fight about it, are determined to conquer the silence, penetrate the mysteries and thus lay claim to a region they would rather die than give up. Moisture in any terms but sweat and saliva is suspect. Niggardly rain taunts and teases. The land punishes native, invader, and even itself it seems. It is the land of the rain shadow—the east side of mountain ranges where moisture pushed by cooling winds is stingy. Yet, Kelton, with words, romances the rain shadow, tells such compelling stories about the Place and the people who inhabit it that we fall under the spell of the forbidding territory. While we suffer and are even repulsed by such a region, we often fall in love with it and make it our own because a great storyteller bids us do so.

Kelton's body of work provides cultural filters through which a reader may view Place. Anglo, European, Plains Indian, Mexican each with wide variety within their ethnic perspectives of gender, age, temperament, work, and way of life matter. Carrying the cultural baggage of their individual history and folklore provides three dimensional folk who act as seines to catch and hold the metaphor of the journey through a particular time period. Transportation in the form of horses serves as yet another filter wherein viewing the land from the back of a horse or from a wagon seat provides the reader a means of traversing the word-landscape; of viewing it from a loftier and better vantage point. The storyteller makes use of all these notions to sell such forbidding territory—his home.

Certainly others romance the Place with not only words, but in art, photography, music and song, films, exhibits, even advertising, giving it like offerings to hold forever the spirit and mystery of Place, the myth and legend. Because people—good and decent, mean and indecent—populate the wasteland, still converge there, a kind of hope and promise prevails even as we watch government, finance, agriculture, and we, ourselves, destroy it one way or the other. Elmer

Kelton recognized it, knew that the end result of Manifest Destiny still at work today turns out to be one more lesson in destruction and annihilation. But that is never the writer's message. Hope springs eternal even knowing that if rain comes can drought be far behind. Against all odds, the brown and withered desert and plains appear Technicolored under his hand.

Now, Elmer Kelton, storyteller emeritus, has converged with the very earth he so knowingly extolled and rests in his bitterly beautiful land. To say that he will be missed is gross understatement. To say that he and his time and place live forever through his words, is hardly hyperbole.

Works Referenced or Cited:

This Bitterly Beautiful Land: A Texas Commonplace Book, 1972; ed. Al Lowman; intro. by Carl Hertzog, color woodcuts by Barbara Whitehead, publishers Holman and Beacham.

Elmer Kelton and West Texas, by Judy Alter, University of North Texas Press, 1988.

Eyes of the Hawk, Forge, 1998.

Bitter Trail, Forge, 1997.

Elmer Kelton, "What's Wrong With Being Different" in *This Place of Memory: A Texas Perspective*; UNT Press, 1992; ed. Joyce Roach.

Texian Stompin' Grounds, 1941, Texas folklore Society publication.

Stand Proud, Forge, 2001.

Man Who Rode Midnight, TCU Press, Afterword Kenneth Davis, 1990.

The Wolf and the Buffalo, TCU Press, 1986, Afterword by Lawrence Clayton, 1980.

Honor at Daybreak, TCU Press, 1991, TCU Press, 2002.

The Time It Never Rained, 1973, TCU Press, 1984.

Sandhills Boy: The Winding Trail of a Texas Writer, Forge, 2007.

The Hewey Calloway Trilogy

James Ward Lee

ELMER KELTON SAYS that his favorite novel is *The Time It Never Rained*, but his favorite character is Hewey Calloway. Hewey, he says, reminded him of all the old "fiddle-footed" cowboys he came to know when he was growing up on the McElroy Ranch. As he writes in the introduction to the TCU Press reprint of *The Good Old Boys*, Hewey was

> *derived from several I knew in my boyhood. I simply moved them back thirty years in time. . . . Cowboys frequently came to the ranch looking for a job. In the 1930s they were likely to be driving a battered old coupe, but in outlook and spirit they were no different from the horseback Hewey." (x)*

Kelton wrote the first of the Calloway novels sitting beside his father's bedside after Buck Kelton had had a stroke. The first chapter came hard, he says, but after a few false starts, "the dam broke and the story came pouring out, much of it unplanned and seemingly spontaneous, from some deep part of the subconscious. I would stare in amazement at words on the paper, wondering where they had come from." (Introduction, ix). The novel appeared in 1978 and won a Spur Award from the Western Writers of America, one of seven that Elmer Kelton won, along with awards from almost every other western association.

Twenty years after *The Good Old Boys* was published, Kelton wrote a sequel, *The Smiling* Country, a story that takes the characters of the first novel four years into the future. And then, in 2002, Kelton came back to the Hewey Calloway story with what literary historians call "a prequel," a strange but satisfactory term that, according to the *Oxford English Dictionary*, dates back only to 1973. The final novel in the Calloway trilogy, *Six Bits a Day*, takes the reader back to early times when Hewey and his brother Walter are just starting out as cowboys. With these three novels we have, in some ways, Kelton's best statement of what it meant to live in the West in the last days of the Cattle Kingdom and the early days of the modern West. The time of the three novels spans the period from about 1890 till 1910. These were years of great change in Texas and the West. From about 1865 until about 1895, Texans trailed cattle north to the railways as the rails moved from Missouri to western Kansas. Then in the waning days of the Cattle Kingdom, farmers and small ranchers moved onto what had been free range and began homesteading four sections of land—2560 acres. These were much smaller tracts of land on what had once been the great open ranges that belonged to whoever could run cattle on them, at least until the open lands began to be sold by the state of Texas to ranchers large and small. These changes altered the West of film and fiction and caused old-time cowmen to rue the passing of what Conrad Richter's novel called *The Sea of Grass*. The unbroken range of native grass began giving way to the nester's plow. Plowing up the grasslands led, in the middle of the twentieth century, to the great Dust Bowl disaster.

Most people who admire Kelton's works assert that *The Time It Rained* ranks as his best work. But not everyone agrees. The late Benjamin Capps told me more than ten years ago that he thought *The Good Old Boys* was Kelton's best. At the time I agreed with Ben Capps, but now I wonder if the three novels that make up the

Hewey Calloway trilogy don't show Kelton at his best. Tommy Lee Jones may agree with Benjamin Capps about the best Kelton novel, for he directed the 1995 film of *The Good Old Boys* and starred as Hewey Calloway. So far, it is the only Kelton novel that has been made into a movie. With Jones as Hewey, Frances McDormand as Eve, Matt Damon as Cotton, the playwright Sam Shepherd as Snort Yarnell, Cissie Spacek as Spring Renfro, and a miscast Wilfred Brimley as C. C. Tarpley, the film is true to the book in every detail. Re-reading the novel and seeing the movie, as I have done several time, persuades me that Elmer Kelton got everything right as he sat at his father's bedside with a legal pad telling Hewey's story—and the story of a changing Texas. He got it right with *The Good Old Boys*, and it seems to be that he continued getting it right with *The Smiling Country* and *Six Bits a Day*.

I think the best way to see the Hewey stories is to consider the three novels as parts of one long work. Maybe in future years some publisher will see fit to join the three into one long epic of the changing West and the passing of a cherished cowboy way of life in a time long past. There are still cowboys and cattlemen today, but they are living and working in ways that Hewey would neither approve nor believe could be possible. Imagine Hewey being astonished at roundups using helicopters or cowboys on motorized four-wheelers.

Read in order of publication, the story, like the classical epics, begins *in medias res*. That is, the first Calloway novel, *The Good Old Boys*, begins in the middle of Hewey's story. That, of course, is the way we first met Hewey Calloway. And we had to wait for the conclusion of his journey in *The Smiling Country* and the beginning of Hewey and Walter as young cowboys in *Six Bits a Day*. I would not argue that reading the volumes in the order they were written is unsatisfactory, but I think if we start all over and consider this as one novel, we can get a somewhat different picture of those "good old boys" who lived east of the Pecos around the turn of a century which seems long past.

First, the plot. If Aristotle is to be believed in *The Poetics*, plot is the outermost concentric circle that contains all the other elements of drama or epic poetry or fiction—of course Aristotle didn't know about narrative fiction. But many have applied Aristotelian criticism to modern fiction, as I plan to do in this essay. If we follow Aristotle's model, we will consider character, theme, setting, atmosphere, diction, and music as parts of plot. It hardly needs to be said that not all critics are Aristotelians, but R. S. Crane and "the Chicago school" made that way of looking at fiction popular several decades ago. Many critics follow the scheme outlined by E. M. Forster in *Aspects of the Novel*. He puts the elements of novels in boxes, each a separate aspect of a work. But look at *The Hewey Calloway Trilogy* (see, I am now italicizing the three volumes as one) from the point of view that Aristotle would have seen this work. The story, and all these characters, and all these themes, and this West Texas setting, and the language that only Kelton could write are a part of a plot that begins somewhere east of the Pecos River and west of the Conchos as "the 1880s were nearing an end" (*Six Bits* 10). Hewey, born in 1878, is nineteen or twenty and Walter a year younger, and before many pages of the novel are past, we begin to see signs of the "nestering" Walter of later years and the Hewey who has no plans ever to be other than a footloose cowboy. Many of the major adult characters—C. C. Tarpley, Grady Welch, Eve, Fat Gervin, Snort Yarnell—are introduced early in the novel, and they grow—or are fixed permanently—as the trilogy goes forward. Walter, who is already a "nester" in Upton County when *The Good Old Boys* opens, is Hewey's sidekick in *Six Bits a Day*. But before we are more than a few pages into the novel, he falls for Eve, found working in Old Lady Pearson's boarding house and serving food to hungry cowboys, whisky drummers, and local bachelors. They are hardly out of the Pecos Country on a trip south of San Antonio to bring back a herd for C. C. when Walter begins to pine for the woman he hardly knows. Hewey does all he can to dissuade him from dreams of Eve and the settled life that will lead to what Hewey is sure will land Walter in the swamps of "uxoriousness." "Strong women made Hewey uneasy. He had a feeling it was their intention to take over the world, if they had not already done so. Some reckless politicians were even talking about letting women vote, a radical notion from Europe or some other foreign country" (*Six Bits* 45). As they drift south,

> *A faraway look would come into Walter's eyes, and not even a clap of thunder could bring him back before he was ready. Hewey would try to distract him by talking about dreams of his own, dreams of being free as a pair of eagles, roaming the West wherever they pleased, visiting the Rocky Mountains, perhaps even wading barefoot in the California surf.* (228)

But the Walter we see now and later is cut from a far different bolt of cloth. He wants the stable life, and he has already found the woman he wants to live it with. Not that there are not times that Walter gives some thought to kicking over the traces and drifting the world with the likes of Hewey and Snort Yarnell. For a moment in *The Good Old Boys* Walter has a hint of what Hewey's free life is like, but his broken leg, brought on by Hewey's recklessness, breaks him of any incipient wanderlust that might have briefly flitted across his mind. The two sons of Walter and Eve, whom we meet when they are sixteen and fourteen in *The Good Old Boys*, replicate the struggle we saw between Walter and Hewey in *Six Bits a Day*. Tommy, the younger, wants to be Hewey, but the older Cotton wants a far different life for himself. He neither wants to be a cowboy nor a nester, but he still wants a settled life, in his case as a mechanic.

Many of the characters seen in the first novel develop or disappear as the trilogy moves on. C. C. Tarpley, who is pushing hard when we first meet him, has, by the second part of the trilogy moved into Upton City, established a bank, and is the largest landowner in the region. The ignorant and bumbling Fat Gervin, who is a completely incompetent cowboy working on C. C.'s ranch and getting in Hewey's way as they trail the cattle from South Texas back to the home ranch, has now married into the Tarpley family and is running the Tarpley Bank. Grady Welch has been stomped to death by a bronc, and Snort Yarnell is still wandering the West like Hewey. In the final part of the story, Hewey has married Spring Renfro, who doesn't appear till volume two, and he and Spring are headed to the Big Bend to manage Jenkins's ranch where Hewey was working when he broke his leg—the event that ended his bronc busting days and put him on the road to a settled life. The ending of the trilogy has most of the plot elements settled: Fat has been bested in a deal that he had tried to manipulate; C. C., who has spent the third volume sitting in Schneider's saloon suffering from self-diagnosed stomach cancer, finds that he only has ulcers and is ready to displace Fat as his manager; Eve and Walter are living on their land unencumbered by debts; and Alvin Lawdermilk, who loved his liquor, has sworn off and is still prospering as a horse and mule dealer.

The main character of all three novels is, of course, Hewey Calloway. He is fully developed, unlike many of the other characters in the novels who are often interesting but never "round" to use E. M. Forster's term. But Hewey we know well, and we know how wrong he is about the world he wants to live in. Wayne Booth in *The Rhetoric of Fiction* says that there is "a secret communion between the reader and the author" (300). In other words, the readers and Elmer Kelton are in league behind Hewey's back. We all know that things are not going to go well for Hewey in the long term. Cotton is right: cars and machines are the future. Eve is right: a settled life is far better than the footloose life of the roaming cowboy. C. C. Tarpley is right when he lectures Hewey when he sees him for the first time in two years, "Well, if you ain't famous, and you ain't rich, maybe you've come home two years smarter. Ain't you about worn the itch out of your feet, Hewey. Ain't you ready to light someplace?" (*The Good Old Boys* 8). We may sympathize with Hewey, as Kelton certainly does, in the fiddle-footed cowboy's desire for a free life, for trips to Mexico and California and the Canadian border. But we know how wrong Hewey is. When Boy Rasmussen falls dead as he is opening a gate, we know how Hewey will end up if he spends his life as Boy has done. Boy may have "pointed them north" in the great days of the cattle drives, but those days are over—or soon will be. But at that point in the trilogy, Hewey is still not ready to settle. His tribute to Boy Rasmussen when he and Walter bring the body to town and gather in Schneider's saloon for what is a sort of a wake shows that Hewey's romantic view of cowboy life is still intact even though everybody else—except maybe Snort Yarnell and young Tommy—see it coming to an end:

> *"Fellers," Hewey spoke gravely, "me and Walter here, we just brought an old-timey cowboy to town. He was old Boy Rasmussen. Now some of you knowed him and some of you didn't. Whether you knowed him or not, you all know the breed. He was followin' the mossyhorns up the trail when most of us was still followin' our mothers around the kitchen. It was him and his kind that beat out the trails and shot at the Yankees and fought off the Indians. It was them fellers that taken the whippin' so me and you could have the easy life we're livin' today."* (GOB 148)

When Hewey rails against the automobile, which, he is certain, will never replace the horse, we—and Kelton—know how that will turn out. Roping the car in Midland, the bit of high-jinks on the part of Hewey and Snort that gets Walter laid up, is fun at the time, but Cotton knows and Eve knows and Walter knows that if all Hewey wants is fun and the occasional wheeligo girl and the nights sleeping under the stars, it can only lead to the fate that befell Boy Rasmussen. Hewey will end up riding the chuck line, drifting from ranch to ranch for a handout until one day he will get down to open a gate and fall dead. He will have to be buried by other "good old boys"—if there are any left. It distresses Hewey when the old rancher Jenkins, who appears for the first time in *The Smiling Country*, arrives in a car. *With a driver!* It turns out that Jenkins's driver, Peeler, is a pretty good cowboy himself when he breaks a bad bronc. But he tells Hewey that life is better behind the wheel of a horseless carriage than perched on "the hurricane deck" of a wild horse. Peeler's story does nothing to convince Hewey that the old days are drawing to a close. But we all know that "the times they are a-changing." By the time of *The Smiling Country* Alvin Lawdermilk has a car. Blue Hannigan, the mule-skinning freight hauler, has abandoned his wagons for trucks. But despite all occasions informing against him, Hewey still longs for the life described in that great bad poem "Lasca":

> I want free life, and I want fresh air;
> And I sigh for the canter after the cattle,
> The crack of whips like shots in a battle,
> The mellay of horns and hoofs and heads
> That wars and wrangles and scatters and spreads;
> The green beneath and the blue above,
> The dash and danger, and life and love.
> And Lasca!

Maybe his Lasca will turn out to be Spring Renfro, but all the "mellay of horns and hoofs and heads" is over for him when the bronc that he insists on riding on Jenkins's spread in the Big Bend wrecks him and breaks his leg. And then he has to return to Upton City in a horseless vehicle. But before that, four years before that, he abandons Spring and the chance to buy the Barcroft place for a chance to head off with Snort Yarnell to go deep into the heart of Old Mexico. Snort makes it sound like Paradise: "It's way down yonder, way down deep. Beautiful country. Not spoiled like this country is gettin' to be, big and wild and wide open. It's like Texas was before they commenced puttin' fences across it and cuttin' it up for farmin'. It's like goin' back to when we was young" (GOB 250).

But the plot involves a myriad of other characters—remember this is an Aristotelian reading of *The Hewey Calloway Trilogy*, as I have chosen to call it. Walter and Eve, Cotton and Tommy, Spring,

Snort Yarnell, C. C. and Fat, Jenkins and Aparicio Rodriguez and Blas Villegas and Peeler the chauffer, Alvin Lawdermilk and Cora and Old Lady Faversham, Blue Hannigan and Schneider and Pierson Phelps the storekeeper, Julio and Sheriff Wes Wheeler and Texas Ranger Len Tanner. This is only a partial catalog of the people who shape the plot that Hewey is the center of. The characters listed all are important largely as they give insight into Hewey and the world he lives in. Walter and Eve try to redirect him more than once. Walter, in volume one of the *Trilogy*, makes it clear that Hewey's way is not for him; that he wants to settle down with a wife and family. Eve, more than anyone, berates Hewey for his wandering ways. She is as hard on Hewey as she is on Walter when Walter shows any signs of independence. Jenkins and C. C. Tarpley, though they employ cowboys to do the work that often leads to disaster, try to steer Hewey away from himself. Peeler, the chauffer, makes fifty dollars a month to Hewey's thirty, and he makes it clear to Hewey that bronc busting is a hard living. When Hewey has made a foolish bet, Peeler, the chauffer, takes off his uniform and proves that he can still ride, but this is probably his last shot a being a "bronc peeler." He is too smart to end up as a stove up cowboy. Cotton is the conscience on Hewey's shoulder—the good angel—who has learned from Eve that there are better ways to live and that Hewey's ways and days are numbered. Even Tommy, star-struck by his uncle Hewey, makes Hewey think again about how he needs to protect his adoring nephew from a life of busting broncs and chasing mossyhorns. Despite Hewey's own bravado, he sees that a person can get hurt or killed—as Skip Harkness does—by riding the rough ones. But Hewey is hard-headed. He won't learn the easy way. Ranger Tanner tells him and Walter early in volume one: "Cowboy life ain't exactly like the storybooks tell it. You're up before daylight and out till dark. You sweat for thirty days to earn a piddlin' wage that you can blow in thirty minutes" (*Six Bits* 14). That sounds good to the likes of Hewey and Snort and Grady Welch. The good life involves riding and living rough and then going into a saloon and spending their pittance on wheeligo girls and whiskey.

The broken leg helps Hewey see what Elmer Kelton is telling us with this plot. As Kelton says in *Sandhills Boy*, there is

> *a solemn aspect seldom given much attention in books ro-manticizing cowboy life. Cowboys do not stay young. They grow old, they get sick, and they die. It's sad to see an old cowboy, too stove up or too ill to continue the active lifestyle he has lived and loved spending his final days wasting away in the terminal boredom of a rented room or lying helpless in a nursing home.* (240)

Or lying dead beside a gate he has got down off his ancient horse to open.

Much of what we see of Hewey and the characters who surround him points us to the theme that this plot explores. It is a theme that shows up in novel after novel by Elmer Kelton. As he writes in the Introduction to *The Good Old Boys*,

> *Hewey Calloway tries to live a life that is already out of its time. He attempts to remain a horseback man while the world relentlessly moves into a machine age. He tries to hold to the open range of recent memory even after the range has been cubed and diced and parceled by barbed wire. He lives in an impossible dream, trying to remain changeless in a world where the only constant is change.*
>
> *Though the story is set in 1906, the problem of dealing with change has intensified with every succeeding generation. Technological and social upheavals have outpaced our ability to adjust. We find ourselves under constant challenge to come to terms with a new and sometimes frightening world we cannot entirely understand.* (xi)

The changes we see in Hewey are reflected in other ways in this trilogy. If we look back at incidents surrounding the trip Hewey,

Walter, and Fat make to South Texas to bring C.C. Tarpley some cattle he has bought from Old Man Dodge, we see the changes that are occurring in the years following the Civil War. On the way to San Antonio, the trio meets Gabe, a former Buffalo Soldier, who travels south with them. At Fort McKavett, an abandoned fort, Gabe tells Hewey, "If it's all the same, I'd like to stick close to you-all. They's got a reputation here for siccin' the dogs on black folks" (*Six Bits* 130–31). When they go in the saloon, the barkeep asks if "the boy" is with them. He refuses him a drink and says of Gabe, "He'll have to get his from the cistern. And he'd better have his own cup, because he ain't drinking from the one out there." Hewey threatens to wreck the flimsy bar and takes back the money he had laid down for drinks. The bartender says, "You three are welcome, but next time leave that darkey outside" (132). When they are in San Antonio, Mrs. Simpson, who cooks for the jail they are trying to get Padgett out of, says Gabe can sit at the table with Hewey, Walter, and Fat, but, she says, "If somebody comes in, you can move back into the kitchen" (167). Maybe this is what the segregationists meant back in the days of *Plessy v. Fergusson* and before *Brown v. the Topeka, Kansas, Board of Education* when they used to argue for separate but equal.

There were few black people in West Texas once the Buffalo Soldiers had come and gone, but there was always some strife between the Mexicans and the Anglos. Not much of that appears in *The Hewey Calloway Trilogy*, but it is impossible to miss the fact that Alvin Lawdermilk's ranch hand Julio sees himself as set apart. When they have the picnic following the windmill raising, Julio takes his plate and goes off by himself. Hewey notices that Eve has given him mostly chicken wings but that Spring has

> *not shorted him on biscuits. Julio did* like *biscuits, especially when he had plenty of syrup to sop them in. Hewey reached up in the cabinet and brought down a bucket of molasses. "Here's the lick, Hooley. Move them biscuits over and I'll pour some on your plate."*

> *He took one of his drumsticks and exchanged it for one*
> *of Julio's wings. "Always was a little partial to the wing," he*
> *said. (GOB 85)*

Later, when Hewey is staying at Alvin's to help break some horses and mules, he shares a bunkhouse with Julio. "To some people this would have appeared an unseemly display of racial equality, but Hewey had a little of the best of it. He slept on a steel cot, while Julio's was a less sturdy one of wood and canvas. The proprieties were met" (120). Hewey is a little ahead of his time in the matter of race and ethnicity, and that also seems to be the case with Alvin Lawdermilk, who treats Julio more like a son than a hired Mexican. Julio helps Alvin keep his whiskey hidden from Cora Lawdermilk and her mother Old Lady Faversham, whose prejudices run deep, not only against Julio but against men, Alvin and Hewey especially. One of the lines added to Tommy Lee Jones's film of *The Good Old Boys* that does not appear in the novel is, "We ought to gut shoot Alvin and leave him for the hogs." I am sure Kelton would have used that line if he had thought of it. One of Jenkins's top hands is Aparicio Rodriguez, who can handle a bronc even better than Hewey, and in Aparicio, we see that in some places, a Mexican is the equal of any Anglo. Even the cook, Blas Villegas, has a place of some honor. (Kelton notes in *Sandhills Boy* that he borrowed the name Aparicio Rodriguez from a soldier he served with in Europe in World War II.)

To fully appreciate the artistry of *The Hewey Calloway Trilogy* it is necessary to consider the setting and see how important it is to the entirety of the novel—the plot, if you will. West Texas is Kelton's home country. He opens *Sandhills Boy* this way: "In Spanish it is *querencia*, in German *Heimat*, the place of the heart, the homeland. For me, it is that part of Texas west of the ninety-eighth meridian. In particular it is a ranch in Crane and Upton counties, just east of the Pecos River" (11). For most Americans, this is country so dry and so barren that it is a part of what old maps used to label "the Great American Desert." It is the country that Walter Prescott Webb defines in his 1931 classic *The Great Plains*. Rain is scarce, and in its better parts, it takes ten acres to sustain one cow; in drier parts it may take as many as a hundred acres per cow. Crops are hard to make without serious fertilizer and irrigation. In the days of *The Hewey Calloway Trilogy*, there was none of the modern irrigation techniques found there today. Nesters had to practice dry land farming. In Kelton's famous *The Time It Never Rained*, the effects of drought are manifest. But even in normal times rain was scarce and grass dried up. It was a hard and unforgiving land, but those hardy souls like C. C. Tarpley and Jessup and Jenkins who helped to settle that land would never have traded it for the lush lands of East Texas or the country that Hewey describes to C. C. early in *The Good Old Boys*. Hewey tells C. C. how he has been everywhere and seen everything—"I've worked cows from the San Saba River plumb up to Wyoming and Montana. I even went north once into Canada and seen the glaciers. You ever seen a glacier, C. C.?" Old man Tarpley tells him, "Them places are too far from here ever to amount to anything" (13). And while Hewey has fond memories of his trips to the rest of the world—even to Cuba during the Spanish-American War—it is to West Texas that he always returns. And it is not just to see his kin. It is his country. He is home in land stretching from Alpine to Fort Stockton to San Angelo. This land makes him feel free, and in the end he and Spring, now married and settled, are going into the Big Bend to manage the ranch that Jenkins had wanted him to manage even before Hewey got crippled up. People who know Hewey, a man of integrity despite his desire to roam, can trust him to manage this land and the people if he says he will. He and Spring will live happily, we hope, working with Aparacio Rodriguez and Blas Villegas and all the hands on the Circle W. Even Snort Yarnell may join Hewey, but, he says, "I got to go get a little drunk first, and I sure do dread it." (*Smiling Country* 253). Elmer may have borrowed Snort's comment from a line Willie Nelson made famous. Hewey tells Spring it is a smiling country out in the West Texas mountains.

For Hewey, for Kelton, for all the characters we meet in the trilogy, the West is a smiling country—plains or mountains or the heart of the Chihuahuan Desert. Place is paramount in this novel and in all of Kelton.

One thing that marks Elmer Kelton's fiction and non-fiction is a wonderful sense of style. His narrative style is plain and unencumbered. He does nothing to call attention to it when he is describing a person or a place or an event. Too often writers get carried away with purple passages and distract the reader. Kelton never does. Note this description Walter renders of old Boy Rasmussen:

> *He remembered the old man now, though it had been some years since he had seen him, and Boy Rasmussen had gone down a long way. The face was pinched and furrowed, the skin dark and dry as old leather. The blue of his eyes seemed almost faded out, so that the red which had rimmed them was dominant. His skin almost touched his nose, for he carried his teeth in a leather pouch hung around his neck, the leather string covered with a once-blue silk bandanna that was faded and dirty and frayed. His hands were shriveled, splotched with liver spots. (GOB 98)*

This is plain style at its very best. There is no editorial comment to heighten the effect, no purple prose to try and make the reader see more than is there. Bad writers struggle to make style stun the reader and end up only disturbing his attention. Poe says somewhere he meant to "heighten the grotesque into the arabesque," whatever that means. I admit that I have never understood exactly what Poe meant, but it can only be bad when it is inflicted on realistic literature. Kelton never does that. He is straightforward and clear. In *The Smiling Country*, he writes:

> *They camped a night besides Fort Stockton's Comanche Springs, where cool, sweet water gushed from the ground in*

a volume that always amazed Hewey. Water was in such short supply across most of West Texas that Nature seemed overly extravagant here. They could have used the likes of this around Upton City. There everybody had to dig or drill for water and could never be certain of finding it. Hewey had seen a driller strike good water, then move fifty feet to one side or the other and come up dry. (90)

Nothing more needs to be said. Emerson either said or should have said that the purely ornamental is never truly beautiful. And Texan Ernest Tubb always told his band, "Keep it low to the ground boys, keep it low to the ground." Kelton always seems to manage to keep it "low to the ground." He is never ornamental in his narrative style, or in his dialog style. When his characters talk, he captures better than almost anyone who has written about life in the West the language used—the slang, the homely adage, the direct assertion. When Tommy comes west and finds Hewey in *The Smiling Country*, Hewey asks why Tommy is not in school.

> "I finished all the schoolin' there was two years ago. I decided to come looking for you."
> "How'd you find me?"
> "Just asked around. Anywhere you've been, they remember Hewey Calloway."
> Hewey tried to sound severe. "You ought to be helpin' your daddy right now. Plantin' time ain't it?"
> "Me and Daddy ain't gee-hawed too good lately. I want to learn to be a cowboy like you."
> "You're too late. They ain't making no more cowboys like me, hardly. The times have gone off and left us." (45)

This is really the way people talk. And who can ask for more from an author is who writing realism?

The language of *The Hewey Calloway Trilogy* is remarkable and unadorned, and it would seem that Kelton is not a writer who indulges in deep—or shallow—symbolism. But there is some to be found here and there. One that strikes me is the biscuit as a symbol for the good life—at least the good life as Hewey sees it. I know. I know. This is stretching things. But I don't think so. Not only is Hewey's horse named Biscuit, and Biscuit has served him well and travels afar with him. And nobody loves a biscuit better than Hewey. Unless it is Julio and Walter and Fat and all the hands on the C. C. ranch and the Circle W and the Jessup spread. In fact, everybody in these three volumes loves biscuits. And they prize anyone who can make one. Remember the scene cited above where Spring piles biscuits on Hewey's plate and says, "You look like a big biscuit-eater to me, Mr. Calloway. How many do you want, five or six?" (85). We also learn that when Alvin is caught with whiskey, Cora Lawdermilk is likely to burn the biscuits, as is Eve. Biscuits and syrup equal plenitude. The good life. Cowboys prize a chuck wagon cook like Blas Villegas who can make good biscuits. Corn bread is poverty. Biscuits are richness.

We are now exactly a hundred years past the time when Spring and Hewey set out for the Circle W, where Hewey is forbidden to ride rough horses now that he is foreman. When we met Hewey and Walter and C. C. and Fat and Snort and Grady Welch it was about 1888, and Hewey was a teenager. In 1906 he is thirty-eight, and now as he and Spring leave Upton City, he is forty-two. He is still a good old boy, but a different and subdued good old boy from the drinker and hell-raiser and chaser after wheeligo girls. Cotton speaks with deep sarcasm when he calls Hewey a good old boy after Walter has been laid up because of Hewey's and Snort's roping the car in Midland. But mostly throughout this long novel, "good old boys" means something different and much better than Cotton meant. When Hewey and Walter bring the body of Boy Rasmussen to town and the boys take up a donation to give him a decent burial and Eve gives up a quilt she has spent hours making for the family beds to wrap him in, even C. C. and Fat kick in to make up a hundred dollars. As

Hewey looks around Schneider's saloon, he raises a glass and says, "To *him*, and to all the other good old boys" (*GOB* 150). If choirs of angels sing good old boys to that smiling country, one hopes they sing "Happy Trails to You," the postlude played at Elmer Kelton's funeral.

Elmer Kelton was a good old boy. "Happy Trails!"

Reading Instead of Roping, Writing Instead of Ranching, and Qualifying for Walrus Hunter: Humor in Elmer Kelton

8

Bob J. Frye

> *Out of all the adversity over the years has come one thing that has always struck me about ranchers and farmers. That is their ability to laugh at their problems. When things are the roughest, and there's no light at the end of the tunnel except perhaps an oncoming train, most of them manage to keep a touch of humor. (My Kind of Heroes 20–21).*
>
> *I take pains to make my settings authentic. Some of you may read Louis L'Amour. He's a nice fellow, and in the backs of his books he has this little piece that says, in effect, 'If I use a spring in my story, that spring exists, I have been there, I have tasted the water, and the water is good.' When I was re-searching* The Wolf and the Buffalo *a few years ago, I started the story on the Double Mountain Fork of the Brazos River. Not to be out done, I went to the Double Mountain Fork, and surely enough, it was there. I tasted the water, and the water was gyppy as hell. ("Address to Friends of the Library Symposium" 10)*

ELMER KELTON HAS CERTAINLY come a long way. From being totally ignored in Larry McMurty's influential essay "Ever a Bridegroom: Reflections on the Failure of Texas Literature" in the *Texas Observer* in 1981, to being voted the greatest Western writer of all time by Western Writers of America in 1995, Kelton has garnered uncommon respect and admiration, including seven WWA Spur Awards for the best Western novel of the year along with the career Saddleman Award and four Western Heritage Awards from the National Cowboy & Western Heritage Museum. Tom Pilkington has asserted that "Elmer Kelton is without question one of the three or four best writers Texas has produced" (*Houston Chronicle* 21 June 2007). It is important to note that when McMurtry's essay was reprinted in 1989 in Craig Clifford and Tom Pilkington's collection *Range Wars: Heated Debates, Sober Reflections, and Other Assessments of Texas Writing*, McMurtry added in a thoughtful postscript to the reprinted essay: "I have a few regrets. One is the omission of Elmer Kelton. I should have read him then, but I didn't. I'm just now reading him. If it's any consolation to Elmer, I'm just getting around to Goethe, too" (40). While *Fifty Western Writers* (1982) includes a thoughtful critical/biographical article on Kelton by Dorys Grover, *A Literary History of the American West* (1987) includes only three brief references to Kelton; *Updating the Literary West* ten years later contains Kenneth Davis's informative chapter on Kelton but the bibliography provides no secondary sources on him. Fortunately, Davis's insightful chapter is complemented by the work of Judy Alter, Patrick Bennett, Lawrence Clayton, Terence Dalrymple, Fred Erisman, Joe Holley, Jim Lee, Joyce Roach, Lewis Toland, and others who have taken Kelton's writings seriously and illuminated his themes, traditions, and artful craft.

What is it that has accounted for Kelton's extraordinary success, especially in recent years? In a word, *authenticity*. Davis has noted not only Kelton's being a "meticulous researcher" but also how his long journalistic experience with the *San Angelo Standard-Times* and the *Livestock Weekly* enabled him to use a spare style "full of carefully chosen details which help create verisimilitude and give the reader an accurate vision of the West" (*ULW* 581). Couple these two Kelton qualities with his personal experiences detailed in his recent memoir, *Sandhills Boy: The Winding Trail of a Texas Writer* (2007), describing his growing up on the McElroy and Lea ranches in West Texas where he was immersed in the realities that actual cowboys daily face and Kelton's willingness to depict these experiences candidly and faithfully—well, then you can see why his readers treasure Kelton's reality over myth, his fiction informed and shaped by actuality over what he calls in his 1980 interview with Bennett the common tendency "to over-romanticize the old-time-cowboy period" (197).

The best single study of Kelton's working in the tradition of the Western yet providing a realistic, authentic depiction of the West is Fred Erisman's "Elmer Kelton's 'Other' West" (1994). Erisman cogently argues that though Kelton began his career in the 1950s writing pulp Westerns in the traditional mode, publishing primarily in *Ranch Romances*, in eight major novels written since 1971 he shifts his focus from the mythic to the mundane West. As he does so, he draws upon the basic materials of the traditional Western, emphasizing land, character, and action, but he tempers them with an empirical knowledge of the actual West gained from his years as an agricultural journalist. The outcome is a substantial body of work very much a part of western literature, yet one that, in its focus upon concrete realities rather than romantic myth, gives the "other" West its due by emphasizing the quiet heroism of the far-from-mythic folk who *really* won the West (291–92).

Kelton himself, in "The Western and the Literary Ghetto" (1983), admits with a humorous, self-deprecating simile that "the pulps were a celebrated training ground for young writers from the 1920s into the early 1950s. Many went on to higher things and hid their shameful past like a parolee who has made a new life" (82).

Kelton's willingness and ability to cut through inflated mythic and extravagant images that lack concrete reality are appealing. Kelton observes: "Superheroes are fun for pure escapism, but when I read I am likely to turn to stories about people who are less than perfect, who have weaknesses, who can make mistakes and be hurt by them, people not quite sure of themselves, characters I can worry over—in short, people like myself" ("Ghetto" 89). "Theirs," Erisman writes, "is . . . a small-scale, democratic heroism" (298); Kelton adds, "To me those are the real heroes. They fight their battles a day at a time. They do the best they can think of, and if that doesn't work, they try something else. Most of all, they hang on and endure" (*My Kind of Heroes* 27), words that echo, it may be noted, William Faulkner's Nobel Prize acceptance speech. These are the stumbling, flawed, ordinary but persistent and courageous folk who call to mind Alexander Pope's description of authentic human beings in his *Essay on Man*—"the glory, jest, and riddle of the world."

I want to pick up on Pope's word *jest*, for what I propose to do initially in this essay is to suggest that humor plays a significant role in the life of Elmer Kelton himself and in the actual lives of the ranchers and farmers he interviews and about whom he writes in both fiction and nonfiction. Indeed, I want to argue that a West Texas humor permeates the very being of Kelton and provides him an authentic, realistic, and artful means for depicting the "other" West effectively.

When Dorothy Parker composed an introduction to the humor of S. J. Perelman, she said, "I had thought, on starting this composition, that I should define what humor means to me. However, every time I tried to, I had to go and lie down with a cold wet cloth on my head" (xii). Defining humor is not easy, but Louis Untermeyer is more helpful:

> *Wit is sudden and startling and usually scornful; it leaps audaciously and wickedly. Humor is slower; it is rarely malicious; it does not fly to assault the mind but laughs its way into the heart. Satire is probing and critical. . . . But humor seldom analyzes; it is warmly sympathetic, playful, sometimes high-hearted, sometimes hilarious. Unlike the poisoned barb of satire and the killing point of wit, humor is healing. It is not only wholesome, but recreative and rejuvenating."* (xvii)

In what follows I want to examine some examples of humor in Kelton's works that laugh themselves into the hearts and minds of his readers. Some seem merely amusing and still others reveal distinct characteristics of West Texas humor—a wry tentativeness, an understatement often phrased in the negative, a deflating, ironic humor, which is frequently self-effacing and contributes to the speaker's *ethos* of genuine modesty, common sense, and a complete lack of pretension.

In addition I want to examine the style and craft of Kelton's humor to see how he makes it effective in a wide range of his writings—memoir, journalism, short stories, novels, coffee table book essays, and speeches. I hope to offer enough illustrations and analyses of Kelton's humor to suggest that it is a significant reason for the appeal that his writings almost invariably have. Finally, I want to stress the therapeutic value of humor here, for Kelton has often written and spoken about the important role that humor has played in helping those pursuing difficult livelihoods—ranching and farming—and facing a challenging, often arid, prickly, sometimes brutal and harsh land where laughter provides a means to cope and endure.

Kelton's memoir, *Sandhills Boy: The Winding Trail of a Texas Writer*, is a treasure-trove of insights into Kelton's personality shaped and honed by West Texas. The book opens with Kelton's unabashed love for that country: "In Spanish it is *querencia*, in German *Heimat*, the place of the heart. For me, it is that part of Texas west of the ninety-eighth meridian. In particular it is a ranch in Crane and Upton counties, just east of the Pecos River. Its proper name is the McElroy Ranch . . ." (11). Kelton admits in his spare style that here "water was scarce, grass was sparse. Most forms of flora and fauna were armed with stickers, thorns, horns, or tusks. Roads were few and . . . prolonged droughts were the rule. . . . It was the last part of the state to be settled, and then only because nothing else was left." Yet he affirms that "it had a wild beauty uniquely its own for those who chose to see it. The lonely expanses offered a liberating sense of freedom. . . . It encouraged quiet contemplation and appreciation for small and transient pleasures like the smell of greasewood after a rain, the distant call of a calf for its mother, even the mournful wail of a coyote on a moonlit night" (12). And how does Kelton respond to dark and suffocating dust storms endemic to West Texas as evident in Quanah native Winston Estes' vivid opening of *Another Part of the House* or Lubbock poet Walt McDonald's revealing lines in his title poem "Whatever the Wind Delivers": "We pretend / we go away by writing French love notes / in dust on the headboard" (22)? Kelton copes with humor. When his Austrian fiancée completes helping his mother clean the ranch house upon her arrival to West Texas, "a sandstorm blew in. Most of their efforts had been in vain, for the doors and windows were not tight. When the wind blew, the curtains billowed even though the windows were closed. Dust settled over everything." Then Kelton adds in a quiet understatement: "Dad commented, 'One good thing, nobody was ever asphyxiated in a McElroy Ranch house'" (SB 188).

Although Kelton grew up on the McElroy and Lea ranches, he did not become an enthusiastic cowboy. He describes his "mediocre record as a cowboy," his failed 4-H Club experience, and claims that the best he could do when he and his competitive roping brother Myrle went to the Pecos Rodeo was to hold Myrle's horse (SB 75–77). Even though Kelton rose to be head cook at the Lea Ranch, he says "my biscuits tended to be flat and shy on flavor, and not to be dropped on a sore toe." Being afflicted with ingrown toenails, he "decided that boots were for vanity, and shoes were for feet" (SB 102). After a fifth-grade teacher had discovered he was nearsighted, he realized why he had had a difficult time keeping up on cattle drives since he had not been able to see the riders on either side of him. (SB 65). So he sought refuge in reading and writing in place of roping and ranching.

His mother had been a schoolteacher and Kelton learned to read by the time he was five. She liked *Ranch Romances*, a Western pulp magazine that sometimes "featured humorous stories by S. Omar Barker about a boy named Mody Hunter, sort of a Western

Huck Finn" (SB 43)—an early influence which would later be quite significant to Kelton. Ridiculed for the results of his lack of good vision, Kelton developed "a serious inferiority complex," admits that "I considered myself a failure, at least as a cowboy," and reading became his refuge (SB 65–66). In addition to the standard classics, he "discovered Texas folklorist J. Frank Dobie, the finely illustrated cowboy-and-horse books by Will James, and the colorful Western adventure novels of Zane Grey. These became a strong influence on the direction my career would take." His wide reading led to "a knack for writing" and he "also discovered an artistic streak. I filled a tablet with drawings of horses and cattle and cowboys" (66). This early interest may explain his admiration for the humor in cartoonists J. R. Williams, Bill Mauldin, and, most especially, Ace Reid, a close friend for forty years (SB 215). Kelton observes about Reid that "what he liked best to draw was cowboys" (215) and at least twice Reid drew one of his stock characters, the hapless rancher Jake, "in a jail cell. One of the names scrawled on the wall was mine" (217).

A dedicated reader and budding writer and illustrator, Kelton excelled in English at school and beat the girls in spelling bees "which in a tough oil-patch town like Crane made me a little suspect" (SB 78). But a significant part of his informal education and an important resource for his later accurate and authentic accounts of ranch and farm life, often employing artful humor, was listening—listening to McElroy Ranch cowboys telling stories, recounting adventures, and spinning yarns. In Bennett's interview with him some twenty-seven years before *Sandhills Boy* was published, Kelton recalls: "I knew a lot of those fellows as old men who had been cowboys in what you'd call the heyday of the cowboy period. I listened to a thousand of their stories when I was a kid" (197). In his memoir Kelton adds:

> As a class, [cowboys] and my father were good storytellers. . . .
> These stories gave me a deep appreciation for history. They
> were about real people of flesh and blood like ourselves, not
> just names in a dry history book. A few of the old men I knew

as a boy had been there during the settlement phase of West
Texas. They had been up the long trails. . . . South of the ranch
headquarters, in the middle of an open pasture, was the grave
of a cowboy killed by horse thieves many years before. . . .
That grave, and stories the cowboys told, awakened a wonder
that stayed with me. They made history come alive. (48–49)

Kelton's wonder-filled listening to yarns and stories encouraged
his writing, not unlike the experience of another Southwest writer,
Rudolfo Anaya. For both authors, listening, really listening, was cru-
cial. In his recent collection *The Essays* (2009), Anaya recalls his
own youth in Eastern New Mexico in "My Heart, My Home," a
1997 essay echoing Kelton's description of West Texas as "*querencia*
[and] *Heimat*, the place of the heart, the homeland" (*SB* 11). His informal learning experience parallels Kelton's, for he writes that "my
role as a writer began in listening to the oral tradition of my community. . . . Tales of the daily life of the people of the Llano Estacado of
eastern New Mexico, their joys and turmoils, became adventures of
the human spirit that held me spellbound" (243). Then in an essay
composed two years later, "Shaman of Words," Anaya adds:

The cuentos reveal moral instruction, joy, humor, insight into
human nature. . . . The time of storytelling . . . sheds light on
the darkness. Those who listen give up their sense of self and
enter into the story. . . . Stories reveal our human nature and
thus become powerful tools for insight and revelation. That's
why my ancestors told stories. That's why I write. (53)

This kind of experience, losing oneself in the story, is precisely
what happened to Kelton when he first started attending school in
the second grade, having skipped the first because of his mother's
homeschooling him (*SB* 42). Kelton writes: "Grade school teachers
conducted a reading hour each day in which they read aloud books
we might not be advanced enough to read for ourselves. When one

started reading *Treasure Island* a bit at a time, I became so enraptured that I badgered Mother into buying me a copy so I could read ahead. It was the first book I ever owned. I still have it" (66).

J. Frank Dobie, one of the major early influences Kelton credits for his becoming a writer (*SB* 66), is described by Francis Abernethy as "a great listener." Abernethy adds that *Cow People*, of which Dobie received advance copies shortly before his death, "is made up of pieces of Dobie's life that he spent sitting in the lobby of Menger Hotel, around campfires, at ranch houses, at meetings of the Old Time Trail Drivers of Texas, just listening" (45).

In his essay in *Celebrating* 100 *Years of the Texas Folklore Society, 1909–2009* entitled "How the TFS Has Influenced Me as a Writer, But More Importantly, What It Has Meant to Me as a Listener," Kelton reinforces Abernethy's and Anaya's words about the importance of listening:

> As a fiction writer I have tried to keep my antenna up for anything that can add color or a sense of reality to my stories. . . . Paul Patterson was one of my high school teachers and remained a lifelong mentor. I always looked forward to a chance . . . to listen to him tell witty stories of his many misadventures as a cowboy. . . . It was my privilege once, during a tribute to Paul, to read aloud his account of a family trip to Midland in a wagon, and his terror on being told that Midland's many windmills sucked up all the air. His older brothers convinced him that they would all be suffocated at the city limits. Paul sat in the audience and laughed as hard as anyone there. (215, 218–19)

Patterson's penchant for humor, clearly evident here, influenced his former student substantially. In fact, Kelton's first significant work in print was his cartoons illustrating "Texas tall tales" in Patterson's *Sam McGoo and Texas Too*. He drew cartoons for a second book by his mentor, *Crazy Women in the Rafters*, but "my artwork did not make the cut. Neither did my career as an artist. I decided it was best to concentrate on becoming a writer" (SB 180); his love of humor could work there.

Kelton kept his antenna up at other conventions, too, like the Western Writers of America. Not having seen regulars James Propp and his wife, Dixie, for several years, he spotted James at a WWA convention in Springdale, Arkansas. He asked him about Dixie:

> *His face fell a little. He said, "I regret to tell you that Dixie died the twelfth of this month."*
>
> *He paused, then added: "I've got her out in the car."*
>
> *Seeing my astonished look, he explained that Dixie had expressed a wish that she be cremated and her ashes buried beside her parents in her hometown, Muskogee, Oklahoma.*
>
> *James complied with her wishes and took her ashes to Muskogee. Unfortunately he arrived on a Sunday and could find no one with whom to make arrangements. So he brought Dixie to the convention, just as he had in the past.*
>
> *I saw him again the following year and asked if he got Dixie buried all right. He said, "Yes, I buried her on the Fourth of July. Dixie always loved fireworks, so I set off some firecrackers at her grave. Ran everybody out of the cemetery." (SB 223)*

The unexpected incongruity in the statement, "So he brought Dixie to the convention, just as he had in the past" and the surprising juxtaposition of firecrackers and a cemetery create humorous effects. In his "Introduction" to his *Book of American Humor* Russell Baker reminds us: "Surprise and freshness are what make humor a delight" (20). Kelton readers can agree.

When Kelton graduated from Crane High School at sixteen, he told his dad he was giving up cowboying and going to study journalism at the University of Texas "primarily," Kelton notes, "because J. Frank Dobie taught there, and I had read all his books. I had *memorized* them" ("Address to Library" 7). Ralph Yarborough reports that

Dobie had been "likened to Will Rogers, Carl Sandburg, and Charley Russell, all of whom he knew. He had a sense of humor second to none of them" (7). It is to be expected that Dobie's style, like that of Paul Patterson, influenced the aspiring writer. Kelton relates that when Dobie first proposed his later famous Southwestern Life and Literature course at the University of Texas, a regent "declared that there was no literature in the Southwest. Dobie was said to have replied, 'There is plenty of life, so I'll teach that'" (*SB* 114).

Once at the university, Kelton learned that his English composition teacher apparently shared the regent's reservations, for he relates that when he was "given an assignment to write a piece on a subject of my own choosing, I wrote about ranch life in West Texas. The teacher gave me a D. She said the writing was acceptable enough, but if I ever wanted to get anywhere as a writer I must learn to choose subjects of importance" (*SB*, 116). This unfortunate experience did not deter Kelton although a imilar experience drove Loren Eiseley away from English into science (*ATSH* 80).[1]

After two years of college and being rejected at seventeen by the navy because of his flat feet, he was drafted into the "walking infantry. So much for military logic," he observes (*SB* 120). En route to Europe on a troop ship, he became extremely seasick—"It was probably just as well that I had not been accepted into the navy"—and afterward he explained in a letter home that he had "made most of the trip by rail" (128), using a pun which is not an especially common source of humor in his writing. Even so, in *Sandhills Boy* he does tell of asking a farmer, Uncle Henry Moore, after he returned from being in the hospital, "what they had done to him. 'Not much,' he said. 'They just drained my purse'" (53).

Kelton escapes wounding or death despite seeing it around him—he told Bennett in his 1980 interview that "I had a few shots fired my way, but it wasn't personal. They were trying to kill me, but it wasn't personal" (195)—and as the war winds down he is assigned to guard prisoners in the Austrian mountains where he meets the love of his life, Anni Lipp. Kelton writes, "Eve hooked Adam with a forbidden apple. I was hooked by [Anni's] forbidden apple strudel" (*SB* 157), for fraternization with the locals was against army regulations.

When Kelton returned to the states to be discharged at Fort Sam Houston in San Antonio, he was provided a list of occupations compatible with his military experience. For a clerk-typist there were many potential jobs and "a great many possibilities were listed for someone who had worked in the motor pool. My classification, however, was rifleman, infantry. The list was short. One item was *walrus hunter*. In later years when I struggled with my writing career, I sometimes wondered if I had missed my true calling" (*SB* 178).

After mustering out, Kelton worked feverishly to find a way to bring Anni from the green forests, mountains, and lakes of northern Austria to the arid, windy plains of West Texas. Finally successful, he met her in New York and they drove back to Texas where she later "learned English by reading the comic pages" (*SB* 190). In an Afterword to *Sandhills Boy*, Anni writes, "As we drove across Texas and the land got flatter and flatter, drier and drier, I am afraid my impression was that we had reached the jumping-off place to hell" (248). She had not yet met the West Texas real estate dealer who described to Kelton a small ranch for sale "pretty much like the McElroy ranch. It's sorry as hell, but it's pretty good" (*SB* 234), and she had not likely heard of Philip Sheridan's famous remark cited by Don Graham in his epigraph to *Lone Star Literature: From the Red River to the Rio Grande*, "If I owned Texas and Hell, I would rent out Texas and live in Hell" ([7]).

Having taken correspondence courses while in Austria and during the summer on his return from Europe, Kelton shortened his time needed to complete his journalism degree following his marriage to Anni and their settling in Austin. While in school he decided "it was time to become serious if I was to be a writer. I bought a grocery sack full of used Western pulp magazines from a secondhand bookstore and studied them, analyzing stories I particularly liked. I dissected them like a frog in a biology lab, trying to unlock

the writers' secrets of construction, description, and characterization. I copied segments on a typewriter to get a feeling for tempo and
the flow of the language. . ." (*SB* 181).[2]

Kelton's persistence paid off—literally—for he sold a story,
"There's Always Another Chance," to *Ranch Romances* before he
graduated. Formulaic like many of his early published short stories,
it contains no humor at all. However, it is after he graduates from
the University of Texas and takes a job as "a farm and ranch writer"
at the *Standard-Times* in San Angelo "where it was cattle for respect-
ability but sheep for a living" that his two writing careers—one as
an agricultural journalist and the other as a writer of fiction—really
take off. Kelton notes that "as my acquaintanceships broadened, I
began to see story characters in many of the people I met. I would
write stories at night and on Sundays, visualizing real people in fictional roles" (*SB* 197).

For the next forty-two years in journalism Kelton kept his antenna up and further equipped himself for moving from formulaic pulp fiction and romantic recreation of the cowboy past to his
own distinctive authentic depiction of the "other" West, one where
humor has a significant role to play. In 1993 the Texas Christian
University Press published *Elmer Kelton Country: The Short Nonfiction of a Texas Novelist.* John Merrill, Director of the TCU Ranch
Management Program from 1961 to 1994 and recipient in 2005
of the National Golden Spur Award, the highest honor a rancher
can receive, says that "by living among [ranchers] and working with
them, Elmer Kelton has learned and recorded far beyond the others.
In terms of birth, upbringing, everyday involvement, he is the real
thing and has been all his life" (*KC* x).

Kelton's humor in this collection is everywhere evident. His
Mark Train-like technique of understated, withheld, added-on surprise—"His roof at night was the open sky, which leaked, of course"
(246); Ozuna's eighty-six-year-old Vic Pierce, on a cattle drive to
San Angelo in his youth "slipped into a West Concho dancehall but
left through a window when shooting started. The window was not

open at the time" (279); a game warden recalled "the hunter who accidentally tied a hard knot at the top of his lace-up sleeping bag and then developed a bad case of diarrhea" (268) — demonstrates the same kind of indirect humor of artfully delayed, wry turns which is so effective in Kelton's novels, especially his later serious ones. Examples of comedy of reversal and ironic parallelism abound. Even the dedication of *Kelton Country* contains an unexpected — and amusing — juxtaposition: "This book is dedicated to my many colleagues in the livestock and agricultural journalism field, who never get considered for the Pulitzer, and seldom even a raise . . ." (xvii). Human foibles, stylistic virtuosity, imaginative combining — all are evident in *Kelton Country*. Such humor can be downright delightful but it can also be therapeutic, healing, recuperative, as Untermeyer has suggested. Humor helps in Kelton country, a demanding environment that requires all who enter it to learn, and learn quickly, how to survive.[3]

Elsewhere I have tried to demonstrate that the humor in Kelton's work is carefully crafted and draws on particular literary traditions.[4] For this present study I will offer some final brief examples of Kelton's uncommonly artful use of humor in *The Buckskin Line* and *Six Bits a Day*.

Then I will close by examining concisely *The Smiling Country* (1998), Kelton's artful sequel to *The Good Old Boys*, and call attention to Kelton's employment of humor in the often harsh, dark, demanding, even tragic world of the cowboy and argue for the importance of the healing, therapeutic quality of cowboy humor.

A number of Kelton's relatively recent novels focus on young characters who develop, mature, and gain understanding and wisdom over the course of the narratives by leaving East Texas for West Texas, just as Kelton's own great-grandfather, Robert Kelton, did in 1878 (SB 17–18). They are *Bildungsromans*, or novels of character formation, a term Kelton likely knew since he told Bennett in their 1980 interview, "I speak a lot better German than I do Spanish," his wife, Anni, being Austrian (201). Jim Ed in *The Man Who Rode*

Midnight (1987), "Trey" McLean in *The Pumpkin Rollers* (1996), "Rusty" Shannon in *The Buckskin Line* (1999), and Hewey Calloway in *The Good Old Boys* (1978) prequel, *Six Bits a Day* (2005), are all young, naïve characters who begin in East Texas and head west to learn ranching and life lessons.[5]

In *The Buckskin Line* it is twenty-one-year-old orphan "Rusty" Shannon who leaves his East Texas farming roots to follow in the Texas Ranger tradition of his foster father, Michael. He will learn ranching from trail boss Ivan Kerbow and find a ranching future with Sarah Stark. Rusty's duty-bound determination to imitate the Texas Ranger tradition of his foster parent, Michael, leads him to become a character almost too good to be credible, as Preacher Webb tells him, "I'm proud of you, Rusty. You were a good boy, and you've grown up to be a good man. Now go and be a good ranger" (123). But Kelton brings Rusty down a notch or two with wry, understated humor when Rusty says that "if James Monahan hadn't come along, I'd have my brains scattered all over the grass." Ranger Tanner observes, "Wouldn't've been enough to make much of a mess" (282). And when the characterization of the Texas Rangers seems to border a little on the "one Ranger, one riot" mystique, as when Capt. Whitfield says to Rusty, "Trouble is what we're here for. We can handle it" (217), more often than not Kelton realistically reveals the tedium, the lack of excitement, of being a Texas Ranger in those early days. Ranger Tanner candidly provides a wry summary of Ranger life: "We get a payday now and again when the politicians in Austin don't spend it all first. Ain't much to waste it on any-way . . . bad whiskey, slow horses, loose women ugly as mud" (143), the assonance of the "u" sound reverberating clearly so that the sound echoes the sense. Kenneth Davis reminds us that "a successful writer of fiction must have a keen eye and a good ear" ("Clio" 20), and Kelton surely does.

In the prequel *Six Bits a Day* Hewey and his brother Walter, en route to escape from an East Texas farm and to gain employment with big West Texas ranch owner C. C. Tarpley, run into Texas

Ranger Len Tanner. Naïve Hewey, the later stumbling hero of *The Good Old Boys*, "judged that Tanner was well into middle age. . . . It crossed Hewey's mind that a ranger must lead an exciting life, maybe better even than a cowboy's. But he did not dwell on the notion long, for he knew he was too poor a marksman to be accepted into such a demanding organization. He could not hit a barn from the inside" (13–14). Here the skilled wordsmith Kelton right away, barely into the narrative, provides Hewey Calloway with a credible, quite appealing character as he undervalues himself immediately through Kelton's typically realistic, understated style. This is the same Hewey Calloway who, in the opening scene of the second installment of the Hewey Calloway trilogy, *The Good Old Boys*, is a drifting, free-roaming cowboy with a rattlesnake skin stretched over the cantle of his saddle widely believed to ward off hemorrhoids which, like rheumatism, were "another ailment common to the horseback profession. Hewey doubted that, because he had them" (3). Thus in these two first installments of the Hewey Calloway trilogy, which confronts uprooting change, greed, prejudice, love, youthful hope, and age's debilitating realities, Kelton utilizes humor as a tool for vivid, realistic depiction of the works' major character, drawing on stories heard as a boy, accounts gleaned as an agricultural journalist, anecdotes listened to attentively at Texas Folklore Society and Western Writers of America meetings, and long experience creating credible settings with authentic conflicts that sometimes are not ever fully resolved by fallible, ordinary human beings despite their uncommon persistence and strength.

The sequel to *The Good Old Boys*, entitled *The Smiling Country*, is set in 1910, four years after Hewey rides off with Snort Yarnell and leaves Spring Renfro behind. Hewey has worked two years as a cowboy on the J Bar Ranch in the "smiling country" of the Davis Mountains of far West Texas for a C. C. Tarpley-like tight, hence rich, ranch owner named Morgan Jenkins. Hewey tutors Skip Harkness and Hewey's nephew Tommy, young cowboys in the mold of Trey McLean, Rusty Shannon, Jim Ed, and young Hewey himself. Owner Jenkins rides in a car driven by a man who earns $50 a month—$20 more than Hewey with all his years of experience— for steering what Hewey calls a "stink wagon." Hewey turns down the foreman's job—too much responsibility—but tutors Skip until Skip is gored fatally, and then takes his nephew, Skip's close friend Tommy, back home to Upton City where he learns of Fat Gervin's dishonest horse sale and plans to trick Gervin and regain his boss's money. While trying to ride, against owner Jenkins' orders, a horse that Tommy cannot handle, Hewey is seriously injured, returns to Walter and Eve Calloway's place to recover, and finally agrees to accept the foreman's job at Jenkins' ranch and marry Spring Renfro.

This brief summary suggests the "darker side" of ranching life: Skip is gored fatally, Hewey breaks his arm and crushes his knee, and he begins, finally, to realize his mortality. Danger, greed, love, deceit, and trouble permeate this sequel even though Hewey and Spring finally do marry and settle down. Hewey's choice is not really a free one; he is aging and becoming limited in what he can do. Even so, there is much humor here. As in *The Good Old Boys*, Kelton again skillfully utilizes three main kinds of humor: comic scenes, tall tales, and the humor of indirection.

Dorys Grover has written that one of the major themes in Kelton's works is "the effect of change upon people and how they meet the challenge of change" (*Fifty* 239). In *The Smiling Country* Hewey cannot tolerate the alterations wrought by the "stink wagons," the trucks and automobiles that his long-time friends freighter Blue Hannigan and rancher Alvin Lawdermilk begin to see as necessary to their businesses. Throughout most of this novel Hewey ignores all the signs around him of his getting older and more vulnerable, flouts J Bar owner Jenkins' specific order that "Them broncs are for the young hands to break. I don't want you ridin' any of them" (26), and consistently engages in self-deception by providing, in response to Dr. Evans' question, "Didn't anybody ever tell you that riding broncs is a job for the young?" his "stock reply . . . whenever a man had a sitting-down job he should hang on to it" (152–53)—a statement drawn directly from the actual words of "an old black horse-man named Albert Merrill" whom Kelton knew (*SB* 209–10). Late in the novel, in what is for Hewey an epiphany, it is Snort Yarnell, so prominent in earlier scenes with his bravado, who "was always alone, Hewey realized . . . It came to Hewey as a sudden revelation that Snort was getting old, too old to continue much longer the kind of life he had led. Hard as he might fight it, trying to live young and loud and reckless, the years were pressing down on him. . . . *Maybe I ain't far behind you*, Hewey thought. A chill ran through him. . . ." (241).

The theme of appearance versus reality—J Bar Ranch owner Jenkins' apparently wimpy automobile driver in fact "rode awhile with Booger Red Privett's bronc show" (43)—permeates this novel. The plot turns, finally, on Hewey's clever tricking of old rancher C. C. Tarpley's mean, deceitful son-in-law, Frank Gervin, who had sold ranch owner Jenkins, Hewey's boss, some sorry stock by pretending they had come from Alvin Lawdermilk's *raising* when, in fact, they had only been driven across Alvin's land so that Gervin could say, quite literally and full of mischief, that they had come from Alvin's place.

While there are five major comic scenes in *The Good Old Boys*, there are really only two principal ones in *The Smiling Country*, one at the beginning of the novel and one at the end. Indeed, the closing comic scene in the book results when Hewey, recovering at his brother Walter and sister-in-law Eve's nester home from his injuries that have ended his bronc-busting days, has "the first stir-rin's of a notion" (235), a scheme to trick banker Frank Gervin into buying back the sorry horses he misleadingly sold rancher Jenkins. The principal actor in this orchestrated maneuver to trap dishonest banker Gervin is none other than the surprising bronc rider Peeler, Jenkins' automobile driver who poses as a rich Dallas cotton buyer looking for a string of horses for his new ranch. Greedy Gervin falls for the bait in hopes of a quick profit. Kelton describes the closing of this final comic scene:

> *Fat Gervin was on his way to look at the horses he had bought, the ones he expected to turn a nice profit for him. Jenkins climbed into his automobile while Peeler cranked the engine. Gervin turned to look as the car pulled away from the front of the [Upton City] saloon. He started to wave, but his hand froze in midair. Hewey wondered who he recognized first, Peeler or Jenkins, and how long it took him to realize they were working together.*
>
> *Gervin staggered back a step. His body seemed to sag. He stared into the dust until the automobile passed out of sight around the livery barn. He slumped onto the edge of the wooden sidewalk, his arms hanging limp. Most people called him Frank to his face. Only a few who had no tact or had nothing to lose called him Fat where he could hear it.*
>
> *Walking by him, Hewey said, "It's been a pleasure to do business with you, Fat." (247)*

This final comic scene provides appropriate closure, for this fat, inept man who had "married up" by winning rich rancher C. C. Tarpley's daughter, who held a grudge against Hewey for helping Walter and Eve avoid bank foreclosure on their farm and about whom it was said, "Around here it was a mark of honor to be disliked by Fat Gervin" (110)—this low-life gets his just desserts.

Moreover, this comic scene connects effectively with the opening one in *The Good Old Boys* where Hewey was taking a bath, uncommon for him, and wearing only a hat—"I sunburn easy," he told C. C. Tarpley when he and his son-in-law drove up in their wagon. Hewey cut right through the social hypocrisy of Upton City folks' calling Frank Gervin "Fat" only behind his back; "Hewey said, 'Howdy, Fat'" (6). Hence the closing comic scene in *The Smiling Country* vividly reveals protagonist Hewey who gains sweet revenge at Fat's expense, finally surrenders to change, and settles down to become both foreman and husband. Connecting seamlessly with the earlier award-winning novel, this sequel's final comic scene produces a victory for Hewey and a triumph of art for Kelton. Perhaps Kelton's interest in John Ford's movies, which Kelton says "I have admired very much" (Grover, "Talking" 42), is pertinent here, for John Cawelti remarks "part of the richness of [Ford's] work comes from the way in which exciting adventure and good-humored social comedy—the dominant themes of *Stagecoach* and *My Darling Clementine*—are inextricably mixed with a subtle feeling of melancholy for a more heroic life that is passing" (247). One kind of humor that Kelton employs to communicate, and confront, this melancholy is comic scenes.

A second principal kind of humor Kelton uses effectively is the yarn, the exaggerated story, the tall tale. He employs fewer "windies" in this sequel than in *The Good Old Boys*, but they clearly contribute to the narrative. They help describe the unique qualities of Upton City where "locals liked to tell gullible city folks passing through that there were so many windmills they sucked up all the wind on slow days and left the air deadstill on the downwind side of town" (*SC* 100)—Kelton, his antenna always up, here draws on a witty narrative about a boyhood experience of his mentor Paul Patterson ("How the TFS" 218–19). When fragrant Snort Yarnell, "an adolescent forever except in years" (*SC* 37), comes to see Hewey to help heal him with his less-than-professional horse medicine practices, Kelton writes that "at the supper table, Lester the nester boy listened with mouth hanging open as Snort told stories. Some contained a grain or two of truth, though not enough to hurt them much" (220). But the best example of how Hewey could spin an exaggerated yarn occurs when green cowboys Skip Harkness and Tommy Calloway are riding through the smiling country toward the Circle W and a roadrunner trots beside them "lettin' the horses scare up dinner for him" (72). When the boys see the roadrunner swallow a frightened lizard, Hewey observes:

> "It would've had better luck if it'd been too big to swallow whole. That paisano bird might've just grabbed it by the

tail, the tail would've broke loose, and the rest of the lizard would've gotten away. They can grow a new tail, you know."

Skip was incredulous. "That story's too big to swallow whole, too."

"It's a fact. Why, I've heard the Mexicans tell about paisanos *that raised herds of lizards like me and you would raise a herd of cattle. They wouldn't eat anything but the tails, and pretty soon the tails would grow back. Them birds didn't have to waste time huntin.' They just laid around gettin' fat and watchin' their herd grow new tails over and over, the way sheep grow a new clip of wool every time you shear them."*

Tommy suppressed a grin; he had heard his uncle spin windies before. Hewey took pleasure in the quizzical expression on Skip's freckled face as the young cowboy floundered between scorn and reluctant belief. It did a green kid good to guess a little, reminding him that he didn't know everything. (73)

This seemingly innocuous yarn actually reveals Hewey, himself the naïf earlier in *Six Bits a Day*, now in the role he fills throughout this sequel—that of teacher. Hewey serves as a role model for the young cowboys and observes as he watches Tommy develop, "Tommy would wish he had a tarp to shed water from his bedroll. Well, next time he would know. Life was one hard-learned lesson after another" (72). And here, in this yarn, Hewey is making it possible for literature, in the guise of a tall tale, to function precisely as Horace long ago in *Ars Poetica* suggested it should—to delight and to instruct. Hewey is trying to teach meaningful lessons to this young greenhorn Skip, whom he earlier derided for being too cocky and self-assured by telling him, "If brag was whiskey, you could open a saloon" (21). Yet all of Hewey's lessons to Skip are for nought, it turns out, for the boy, foolishly self-confident, dies on the horns of an angry bull he baited. Maybe Tommy will be a better pupil.

The final kind of humor considered in this novel takes

many forms—the humor of indirection. Sometimes it is delightful sentence-ending surprise that merely evokes a smile as when Hewey responds to Eve's advice not to alienate banker Gervin since he still holds the mortgage on their place and Hewey replies: "The only reason Fat's a banker is that C. C. Tarpley says so. But I'll watch myself. I'll bend over backwards to be nice to the son of a bitch" (99).

The irony may be artfully designed to catch us unawares as when Alvin, a recovering drunk, suggests injured Hewey pray but then learns from Hewey that Fat Gervin has driven sorry horses over his land twice to try to defraud buyers: "Alvin swore: 'The duplicitous son of a bitch!' Hewey was surprised to hear such language come from Alvin. He didn't used to say words like *duplicitous*" (214). Often this humor helps with characterization. When Kelton wants to portray a tight-as-bark-on-a-tree rancher like Tarpley, his narrator wryly remarks: "He never liked for a cowboy to see the sunrise through a window, or the sunset either" (117). Snort Yarnell, whose character is revealed well in the earlier novel when he relates how he wrapped his broken leg in horse manure to hasten its healing, remains consistently fragrant in the sequel: "'Snort Yarnell!' Hewey shouted back. 'Somebody told me you was dead. Guess you just smelled like it'" (36).

Kelton is equally at home with understatement—"Eve had a way of making him [Hewey] feel guilty even when he was as innocent as a newborn calf. It almost ruined his appetite, for he refilled his plate only once and didn't eat but six biscuits and two helpings of dried-apple cobbler" (100)—an ironic Swiftian juxtaposition: the narrator describes how C. C. Tarpley "cut out a goodly chunk of range for himself and held it against cattle thieves, drought, lawyers, bankers and other hazards of the ranching trade" (105). Moreover, there is sheer delight in listening with our post-modern ear, the one without the cell phone pressed to it, as freighter Blue Hannigan speculates in 1910: "The day'll come when you'll stand at the road and see a car or a truck pass by every ten or fifteen minutes. Horses and mules are fixin' to go the way of the buffalo" (183).

It is clear, then, that in Kelton's recent novels in the *Bildungs-*

roman tradition and, more particularly, in his sequel to *The Good Old Boys*, humor in a wide variety of forms plays a significant role in his delightfully distinctive style. He seems to be following in the tradition of his mentor, S. Omar Barker, whose humorous stories he had read in *Ranch Romances*. Of Barker Kelton observes: "Omar's fiction almost always had a touch of humor, which I found refreshing. Too many traditional Westerns have been gray in mood and humorless" (SB 221). Yet alongside almost all of Kelton's own humor is a deep sense of sadness and tragedy and despair.

In "My Kind of Heroes" he advises us: "Listen hard to an oldtimer's humorous stories about better days and you'll usually find there was a certain amount of pain and anxiety that seems a lot funnier now in the telling than it did when it happened" (12–13). Then he adds, "My dad told me the history of a lot of the ranches and ranch operators in the Midland-Odessa country. He knew most of them and cowboyed for a lot of them in his youth. No matter how funny Dad's story was, it usually tended to end on a sad note" (15). When Bennett suggested that *The Time It Never Rained* "paralleled the Book of Job," Kelton replied, "I didn't plan it, but . . . it . . . seeped into my consciousness that here was Job, updated" (200). To Bennett he also admits to looking at "the darker side of life" in his comic masterpiece *The Good Old Boys* (192), and in his "Introduction" to its TCU edition he explains that while he intended for it "to be a humorous and good-natured look at West Texas country life of that period," he "wrote in sadness, a lament for a less-pressured time and a simpler way of life that had died, as my father was dying" (xi). Commenting on his father's death at seventy-eight after his having spent some thirity-six years on the McElroy Ranch, Kelton in his memoir candidly observes: "This is a solemn aspect seldom given much attention in books romanticizing the cowboy life. . . . It is sad to see an old cowboy, too stove up or too ill to continue the active lifestyle he has lived and loved, spending his final days wasting away in the terminal boredom of a rented room or lying helpless in a nursing home" (SB 240). Kelton illustrates, in his "Foreword" to

Red Steagall's poetry and songs, "the loss of open-range days and ways, and the tragedy of a confining old age for cowboys" by citing Steagall's lines: "I stood by the fountain as they brought him in. / A lost lonely look on his face. / I ain't never seen him in nothin' but boots. / The wheelchair shore seemed out of place" (7).

Kelton's approach in his own fiction, a realistic commingling of comedy and melancholy, is entirely appropriate, for Wiley Sypher has reminded us that "tragedy needs a more single vision than comedy, for the comic perception comes only when we take a double view—that is, a human view—of ourselves, a perspective by incongruity" (*Comedy* 255). Kelton creates that human perspective which often functions as a coping mechanism; as Untermeyer informs us, humor is not only healing and wholesome "but recreative and rejuvenating" (xvii) as well. The difficulties, the adversities, the tragedies of real ranchers and real farmers were all mitigated by them with saving humor. C. L. Sonnichsen provided in 1988 a view of *The Laughing West*, and Max Evans in his foreword to Sonnichsen's *Final Harvest and Other Convictions and Opinions* (1991) writes of being raised on cow ranches and the role of humor there: "No matter how broken-boned and broken-hearted the lives of these old cowboys were; no matter how bent, scarred and debased their entire lives had been; they found it possible to laugh at its ridiculousness. . . . The kind of humor emanating from our 'vanishing West' . . . became an art of survival over and over . . ." (ii).

Ernestine Sewell reminds us in "The Humor of Westering Women; or, She Who Laughs, Lasts" that pioneering women, too, facing enormous hardships, drew on wit for strength (108, 113), practicing what Sonnichsen calls in *The Laughing West* the "saving sense of humor"(qtd. in Evans iii). Kelton's artful humor helps him accurately depict the genuine "other" West, to borrow Erisman's phrasing; he combines comedy and tragedy so effectively that he is able fulfill his own description of the goal of literature: "Though the primary purpose of fiction has to be to entertain, it can also illuminate and explain" ("Truth of Fiction" 71).

Near the conclusion of *The Man Who Rode Midnight*, green-horn Jim Ed from Dallas learns perhaps his most significant lesson. His wizened grandfather Wes asks Jim Ed to accompany him back out to Lubbock in West Texas and his family's old home place. Jim Ed hears the sad tales of some of his granddad's cowboying cohorts—Grover Cleveland Ransome and Ol' Snort Yarnell and Ol' Brewster Downing, the last "in a nursin' home down in Lubbock . . ." (240). All the while, Jim Ed is watching, seeing, learning. He gains insight into what it means to be a human being, a human being moving inevitably toward decrepitude—like Boy Rasmussen in *The Good Old Boys*, a literary parallel to those coming to an end depicted in Frederick Remington's *The Fall of the Cowboy*. It is a lesson with a long literary history: from Juvenal's "how grisly, how unrelenting / Are longevity's ills" ("Satire X" 190–91), to Shakespeare's "second childishness and mere oblivion, / Sans teeth, sans eyes, sans taste, sans every thing" (*As You Like It* 2.7), to Jonathan Swift's pathetic Struldbruggs who combine "all the usual disadvantages [of] old age" with "the dreadful prospect of never dying" (*Gulliver's Travels* bk. 3, ch. 10). Jim Ed is learning, genuinely learning, why his grand-dad has hung on so tenaciously to his land, clung so persistently to his way of living and moving and being. And so, always with a heal-ing sense of humor even under trying circumstances, Kelton helps us, his readers, learn too.

Perhaps, then, we should not be surprised when Kelton tells us, "My stories tend to end bittersweet at best" ("Ghetto" 89). And so, it turns out, must this essay as well. On Friday, December 13, 2002, my colleagues gave me a party on the occasion of my retiring after thirty-seven years at Texas Christian University. It was extravagant and unnecessary and wonderful all at once. Yet the day before, I had learned of the serious illness of a former graduate student in my Lit-erature of the American Southwest class who had earned his Master of Liberal Arts degree yet continued taking MLA classes to enhance his liberal education. So at my gathering I asked my friends please to remember Bill Haines in whatever way they considered appropriate.

The following Thursday I was shocked to read Bill's obituary in the morning *Fort Worth Star-Telegram* and learned there, to my surprise, that I was an honorary pallbearer.

On Friday evening, 20 December, I attended a visitation at Greenwood Funeral Home in Fort Worth. I got there early, and while I usually avoid viewing the deceased, few were around and so I walked over to the casket. I was startled and amazed to see that there, cradled under his right arm, was Bill's copy, from my class, of Elmer Kelton's *The Good Old Boys*.

Back home I dug out an e-mail from Bill dated 13 September 2002 in which he announced the necessity of his withdrawing from one of my colleague's MLA classes. He noted that

> *after three years of undergraduate study and five years of un-interrupted MLA studies, my assignment at work [Lockheed/ Martin] has been elevated to the point where I must travel internationally and extensively. The current world situation has created an environment within the workplace for a few that necessitates extraordinary hours and personal sacrifice — hopefully for a positive purpose. . . . My five years within the MLA structure have been 'cutting edge'. . . . And Mr. Elmer Kelton continues to write; I've even gotten Danes to start read-ing* The Good Old Boys. *Additionally, without my MLA I would not have been elevated to Director of Procurement-F-16 Programs. My studies at TCU have provided a mind-stimulating experience enabling me to decide against retire-ment after some thirty-five years, but instead to continue and attempt to force positive change within the military/industrial bureaucracy. My attempts to insert a Liberal Arts perspective into the workplace logic [are] never-ending. . . .*

Perhaps this experience is why this examination of humor in the writings of Elmer Kelton has been uncommonly difficult yet one of the most rewarding I have ever tried to compose. Perhaps this experience helps explain why I firmly believe that Kelton's writings, informed and shaped in particular by his wide range of ranching and farming experiences and imbued by his distinctive style of West Texas humor, should be taken seriously. Elmer Kelton rewards our attentive reading and cultivates our humanity. And we can be eternally grateful that he chose reading over roping, and writing over ranching and walrus hunting.

NOTES

[1]See *All the Strange Hours*, p. 80. Falsely accused of plagiarism, Eiseley nevertheless became the author of the classic *The Immense Journey* and other distinguished publications. Later he was selected Provost of the University of Pennsylvania, and then was named Benjamin Franklin Professor of Anthropology and the History of Science there. As my West Texas father would say with his tentative highest praise, that was not too bad.

[2]Here Kelton was working in the ancient classical rhetoric tradition of imitation, recommended by Dr. Samuel Johnson (*Boswell's Life of Johnson*, 161) and practiced by Benjamin Franklin (*The Autobiography of Benjamin Franklin*, 61–62).

[3]It should be noted that Kelton clearly has developed the mature discipline to limit his use of humor when appropriate. See his thirteen essays in *Texas Cattle Barons* (1999) addressing the history, challenges, and demands of big Texas ranches with only two brief instances of humor, pp. 87 and 90. See also Lewis Toland, "Guest Editor's Introduction: 'Go Forth and Sin No More,'" 5 (on *Llano River*, a Western farce). On Kelton's farces, see Bennett, p. 183, and Kelton, "Address to Friends of Library Symposium," p. 14 (on *Joe Pepper*). For an early example of Kelton's "working himself toward . . . the wry humor of *The Good Old Boys*," see Judy Alter's "Afterword" to *Wagontongue*, pp. 238–39.

[4]As a student of Kelton's fiction, I have focused on his use of humor in his novels. In 1984 I examined, in a special Kelton issue of *Southwestern American Literature*, three principal kinds of humor in *The Good Old Boys* (1978)—"the comic scene" in the tradition of movie director John Ford, "the tall tale, and the humor of indirection" (17). In 1997 I argued in "The Shaping Spirit of Comedy: Humor in Elmer Kelton's *Honor at Daybreak*" (1991) that Kelton's use of several hyperbolic stock characters, like Robert Flynn's characters in his parody of the trail drive novel, *North to Yesterday* (1967), draws on the Ben Jonson "comedy of humors" dramatic tradition as Kelton employs humor to "develop his serious theme of adjustment to change and finally produces an affirmative work which delights more than it instructs" (79); and in another special Kelton issue of *Southwestern American Literature*, I contended that "in addition to the six drought jokes Kelton incorporates

into his novel, he uses three principal kinds of humor in *The Time It Never Rained*: (1) comic scenes, (2) understated humor, and (3) indirect humor (34).

⁵On Kelton's use of this tradition in *The Man Who Rode Midnight* and *The Pumpkin Rollers*, please see my article "Go West, Young Man, into Maturity: Elmer Kelton and the *Bildungsroman* Tradition," *Concho River Review* 15.1 (Spring 2001): 51–67.

LIST OF WORKS CITED

Abernethy, Francis Edward. *J. Frank Dobie.* Austin, TX: Steck-Vaughn, 1967. Southwest Writers Series 1.

Alter, Judy. Afterword. *Wagontongue.* 1972. By Elmer Kelton. Fort Worth: Texas Christian University Press, 1996. 231–39.

Anaya, Rudolfo. *The Essays.* Norman: University of Oklahoma Press, 2009. Chicana & Chicano Visions of the Americas 7.

Baker, Russell. Introduction. *Russell Baker's Book of American Humor.* Ed. Russell Baker. New York: Norton, 1993. 15–23.

Bennett, Patrick. "Elmer Kelton: Racial Friction Out West." *Talking with Texas Writers: Twelve Interviews.* College Station: Texas A&M University Press, 1980. 179–203.

Boswell, James. *Boswell's Life of Johnson.* London: Oxford University Press, 1953.

Cawelti, John G. "The Western: A Look at the Evolution of a Formula." *Adventure, Mystery, and Romance: Formula Stories as Art and Culture.* Chicago: University of Chicago Press, 1976. 192–259.

Davis, Kenneth. "Elmer Kelton." *Updating the Literary West* 580–84. Cited as *ULW.*

_____. "Kelton's Clio: The Uses of History." *Southwestern American Literature* 27.2 (Spring 2002): 19–25. Cited as "Clio."

Eiseley, Loren. *All the Strange Hours: The Excavation of a Life.* New York: Charles Scribner's Sons, 1975. Cited as ATSH.

Erisman, Fred. "Elmer Kelton's 'Other' West." *Western American Literature* 28.4 (February 1994): 291–99.

Evans, Max. Foreword. *Final Harvest and Other Convictions and Opinions.* By C. L. Sonnichsen. El Paso: Texas Western Press, 1991.

Franklin, Benjamin. *The Autobiography of Benjamin Franklin.* 2ⁿᵈ ed. New Haven: Yale University Press, 2003.

Frye, Bob J. "Car-Roping, Tall Tale-Telling, and Finding Direction Out by Indirection: Humor in Elmer Kelton's *The Good Old Boys.*" *Southwestern American Literature* 9.2 (Spring 1984): 16–29.

_____. "The Shaping Spirit of Comedy: Humor in Elmer Kelton's *Honor at Daybreak.*" *Concho River Review* 11.2 (Fall 1997): 76–90.

_____. "'Sorry as Hell but Pretty Good': Humor and the Sense of the Southwest in Elmer Kelton's *The Time It Never Rained.*" *Southwestern American Literature* 27. 2 (Spring 2002): 27–38.

Grover, Dorys C. "Elmer Kelton." *Fifty Western Writers.* Ed. Fred Erisman and Richard Etulain. Westport, CT: Greenwood P, 1982. 237–45. Cited as *Fifty.*

_____. "Talking with a Texan." *English in Texas* 13.2 (Winter 1981): 39–43. Cited as "Talking."

Kelton, Elmer. "Address to Friends of the Library Symposium. Texas Tech University, Lubbock, Texas. October 10, 1985." *Living and Writing in West Texas* 5–15.

_____. *The Buckskin Line.* New York: Forge, 1999.

_____. *Elmer Kelton Country: The Short Nonfiction of a Texas Novelist.* Fort Worth: Texas Christian University Press, 1993. Cited as *KC.*

_____. "Essays." *Texas Cattle Barons: Their Families, Land and Legacy.* Berkeley, CA: Ten Speed Press, 1999.

_____. *The Good Old Boys.* 1978. Fort Worth: Texas Christian University Press, 1985. Texas Tradition Series 1.

_____. "How the TFS Has Influenced Me as a Writer, But More Importantly, What It Has Meant to me as a Listener." *Celebrating* 100 *Years of the Texas Folklore Society* 1909–2009. Ed. Kenneth L. Untiedt. Denton, TX: University of North Texas Press, 2009. 215–20.

_____. *Living and Writing in West Texas: Two Speeches by Elmer Kelton.* Abilene, TX: Hardin-Simmons University Press, 1988.

_____. *The Man Who Rode Midnight.* 1987. Introduction by Kelton; Afterword by Kenneth W. Davis. Fort Worth: Texas Christian University Press, 1990. Texas Tradition Series 14.

_____. *My Kind of Heroes: Selected Speeches by Elmer Kelton.* Austin, TX: State House Press, 1995.

_____. *Sandhills Boy: The Winding Trail of a Texas Writer.* New York: Forge, 2007. Cited as *SB.*

_____. *Six Bits a Day.* New York: Forge, 2005.

_____. *The Smiling Country.* New York: Forge, 1998. Cited as *SC.*

_____. "The Truth of Fiction." *My Kind of Heroes* 58–74.

_____. "The Western and the Literary Ghetto." *The Texas Literary Tradition* 82–94. Cited as "Ghetto."

Lone Star Literature: From the Red River to the Rio Grande. Ed. Don Graham. New York: Norton, 2003.

McDonald, Walt and Janet M. Neugebauer. *Whatever the Wind Delivers: Celebrating West Texas and the Near Southwest.* Lubbock: Texas Tech University Press, 1999.

McMurtry, Larry. "Ever a Bridegroom: Reflections on the Failure of Texas Literature." *Texas Observer*, 23 October 1981: 1, 8–19. Rpt. in *Range Wars* 13–41.

Parker, Dorothy. Introduction. *The Most of S. J. Perelman*. By S. J. Perelman. New York: Simon and Schuster, 1958. xi-xiv.

Pilkington, Tom. "Voice of Cowboy Sounds Throughout Elmer Kelton's Memoir." *Houston Chronicle* 21 June 2007, p. 19. Chron.com. Web. 1 May 2010.

Range Wars: Heated Debates, Sober Reflections, and Other Assessments of Texas Writing. Ed. Craig Clifford and Tom Pilkington. Dallas: Southern Methodist University Press, 1989.

Sewell, Ernestine. "The Humor of Westering Women; or, She Who Laughs, Lasts." *Myth and Voice of Texas Writers: A Festschrift in Honor of Joe D. Thomas*. Ed. William E. Tanner. Arlington, TX: Liberal Arts Press, 1991. 103–15.

Sypher, Wylie. "The Social Meanings of Comedy." *Comedy*. Garden City, NY: Doubleday, 1956. 241–55.

The Texas Literary Tradition: Fiction, Folklore, History. Ed. Don Graham, James W. Lee, and William T. Pilkington. Austin: College of Liberal Arts and the Texas State Historical Association, 1983.

Toland, Lewis. "Guest Editor's Introduction: 'Go Forth and Sin No More.'" *Southwestern American Literature* 27. 2 (Spring 2002): 5–7. Special Elmer Kelton Issue.

Untermeyer, Louis. Introduction. *A Treasury of Laughter*. New York: Simon and Schuster, 1946. xvii-xix.

Updating the Literary West. Ed. Thomas J. Lyon and others. Fort Worth: Texas Christian University Press, 1997. Cited as *ULW*.

Yarborough, Ralph W. *Frank Dobie: Man and Friend*. Washington, D.C: Potomac Corral of the Westerners, 1967. The Great Western Series 1.

Elmer Kelton Speaks Out . . . On the History of the Western Novel

9

Elmer Kelton

At a meeting of the Chisholm Trail Roundup Writers' Workshop on the TCU campus in June of 1990, the crux of the meeting turned on Patricia Limerick's view of the American West contrasted with Elmer Kelton's. Professor Limerick, one of the leaders of the "New West Historians" made the case outlined in her book Legacy of Conquest *that the real history of the West had been disguised by generations of historians, western fiction writers, Hollywood movie makers, and folklorists. Her thesis is that "Indians, Hispanics, French Canadians, and Asians were at best supporting actors and at worst invisible. Nearly as invisible were women, of all ethnicities" (*Legacy *21). She made the point that writers, presumably like Kelton, had written volumes extolling the virtues of white males as pioneers and conquerors of the frontier. The concept of Manifest Destiny was a story of white males who tamed the land, drove off the Indians, and in effect ended the frontier that Frederick Jackson Turner wrote about in 1893. But the real story of the West is really a story that includes the women, the Chinese railroaders, the Hispanics, and other ethnicities. The legend of the white male conqueror is a story that captured the imagination of filmmakers, novelists, and*

123

folklorists. The real story of the West is only now being "re-vised" by the New West Historians.

The following article, published in the winter 1989 issue of The Roundup Quarterly, *is based on Elmer's comments at the Chisholm Trail Roundup and reveals much about his approach to dealing with history in fiction.* Editors

Elmer Kelton Speaks Out . . .
Roundup Quarterly
New Series, Vol. 2, No. 2
Winter 1989
On the History of the Western Novel

THE WESTERN HAD ITS BEGINNINGS with the "penny dread-fuls" of Ned Buntline and others in the actual frontier period. It could be said to go back even to David Crockett and his almanac and the frontier tradition of the tall tale. But it really began to take on form with the Buntline period. These were usually tall tales of daring and heroism written about real people such as Buffalo Bill Cody and Wild Bill Hickock [*sic*].

They were almost always written by easterners, not by western-ers. They were usually highly sensational, wildly implausible and heroic beyond all reason.

They were also considered not respectable. In general, in polite literary circles today, the western is *still* not considered respectable. Unfortunately for us, we inherited too much from Ned Buntline. If you write a novel that is construed to be a western, no matter how good it is, it has two strikes on it before it ever goes to the plate.

The traditional western as we know it today more or less crys-tallized just after the turn of the century with Owen Wister's *The Virginian.* That book, in its time, was considered *highly* respectable. It was fresh and new, a great departure from the penny dreadfuls. It had a literary polish nobody had given the western before.

It seems old-hat and clichéd today. That's partly because literary styles have changed, and partly it's because so many westerns since have picked up and repeated so much from it.

Too many western heroes have been the Virginian with a different name. Too many western heroines have been Molly the school-teacher without much change except that she is Mary or Jane, and she may be the rancher's daughter. Too many main-street shootouts have been a replay of the Virginian and Trampas. Much, much too often, western novelists have gone back not to actual history but to Owen Wister.

It isn't always that they have intended to. I suspect there are western writers today who haven't even read *The Virginian*. But they have read and patterned their work after other western writers who did and do.

What's more, through the years this trend has been fostered and encouraged by publishers and by Hollywood. The West as they envision it often comes closer to *The Virginian* than to reality. They are most comfortable in this semi-mythical setting and don't like to be troubled by deviation from it.

I've forgotten the writer's name, but there was one young fellow soon after World War II who became very prolific and very popular for a while in the pulp magazines, then disappeared. What happened was, he gave up. He wrote an article for a writers' magazine and complained about the rigid mold into which the western had arbitrarily been frozen. He said the editors all want you to write something different, but keep it the same.

In those days the hero had to be what the name implies: A *hero*. He might be given to a little self-doubt and introspection but never enough to hurt him. In the end he always had to win out against overwhelming odds simply because he was the better man.

The heroine was under even tighter restrictions. She was usually expected to be dependent upon the hero and never, *never* outdo him.

In my first full-length novel, *Hot Iron*, back in the mid-1950s, I had the villain trap the hero and have him at his mercy, defenseless.

The heroine—in my version—picked up a pair of scissors and ran him through, saving the hero.

The editor changed that. He let the heroine use the scissors, all right, but that only provided a momentary distraction which let the hero grab his pistol and kill the villain himself.

In general, in those days, an editor would rather see a heroine faint than fight. They've changed some today.

The late Stephen Payne was a Colorado cowboy who started writing for the pulp magazines back in the early 1920s. He said the main function of the heroine in a western was to be chased and chased, but to remain ever chaste. Fortunately we see publishers today willing to let women be strong and sometimes even dominate a story. Witness Judy Alter's novel *Mattie*.

They'll also allow a lot of deviation from the old strong, silent Anglo-Saxon hero. I've written two novels in which the lead characters were black, and one in which the principal character was a Mexican cowboy. They were published.

A few years ago Doubleday had a series of westerns by the late John Reese featuring as their main character a Jewish peddler, Sure-Shot Shapiro. Back in the pulp magazine days even the mailbox would have rejected a story like that. It would have pushed the manuscript back into your hands.

Most western publishers today like a story well grounded in history. They like authenticity, or at least the *Air* of authenticity. Many editors don't really know a lot about the West. Some writers put a lot over on them by making it *sound* right. But in the long run, readers have a tendency to weed out the ones that play fast and loose with reality.

I think one reason for the phenomenal success of Louis L'Amour was that he at least gave his books a feel of authenticity. You might quarrel with him on details, but in the main his books at least painted a consistent picture of a West as he saw it, and he built a following that the rest of us can only envy. I appreciated him because he represented the western genre well, wherever he went. He was good for the western.

Unlike a few others I have seen or known about, he never downgraded other western writers. He never claimed that his was literature and the rest was trash. He never apologized for being a western writer. He claimed that a good western is a good novel and therefore just as worthy as a good mystery or a good piece of science fiction.

I agree a hundred percent.

He fought a losing fight with the critics, of course. Eugene Manlove Rhodes lost that fight sixty years ago, and he was one of the most literate of all the western writers. He did not do formula westerns, but he was lumped with those who did, and he bitterly resented being brushed off by the eastern critics. He was unable to beat the system. Louis L'Amour never beat it. Neither, likely, will any of us.

Now and then you'll find a book about the West that gets the approval of that class of critics, but as likely as not it will be a book which sneers at or condemns what we used to call "the winning of the West." Very often such books are written by people who know a lot less than they think they do, or claim to know, about the subject. They write from the standpoint of modern mores, and they tend to condemn our forefathers for not having our modern, enlightened and ennobled outlook.

These kinds of books sometimes—not always—win a certain popularity among segments of the buying public who do not ordinarily read westerns. But as a rule you'll find that the real western-buying public resents and rejects them. They recognize that this modern type of "instant history" is as fraudulent in its own way as the highly-stylized old powder-burner pulp western ever was.

The people of the Old West were neither the eight-foot-tall heroes of the old pulps nor the greedy, grasping, violently prejudiced villains who usually people the books done by the professional ancestor-haters. There were our fathers and grandfathers and great grandfathers. In many ways they were like us. They had many of the same problems, the same fears and certainly the same emotions that we feel today.

Too many today would judge our forebears by today's standards, not by those of the times in which they lived. How will we fare a hundred years from now if we are judged by the standards that prevail *then*, rather than by the ones under which we live today?

A Basic Bibliography of Books by Elmer Kelton

Compiled by Felton Cochran
of The Cactus Book Shop
San Angelo, Texas

NOVELS:

1956 *Hot Iron
1956 *Buffalo Wagons [Spur Award]
1957 *Barbed Wire
1959 *Shadow of a Star
1960 *Texas Rifles
1961 *Donovan
1962 *Bitter Trail
1963 *Horsehead Crossing
1965 *Massacre at Goliad
1966 *Llano River
1967 *After the Bugles
1969 *Captain's Rangers
1969 *Shotgun Settlement (Written as Alex Hawk)
1969 *Hanging Judge
1971 *Bowie's Mine
1971 The Day The Cowboys Quit [Spur Award]
1972 *Wagontongue
1973 The Time It Never Rained [Spur Award; Western Heritage Award]
1974 *Manhunters

1975 *Joe Pepper* (Written as Lee McElroy)

1976 *Long Way to Texas* (Written as Lee McElroy)

1978 *The Good Old Boys* [Western Heritage Award; also filmed for TNT Television]

1980 *The Wolf and the Buffalo*

1981 *Eyes of the Hawk* (Written as Lee McElroy) [Spur Award]

1984 *Stand Proud*

1985 *Dark Thicket*

1987 *The Man Who Rode Midnight* [Western Heritage Award]

1989 **Sons of Texas: Book I*

1989 **Sons of Texas: The Raiders*

1990 **Sons of Texas: The Rebels*

1991 *Honor at Daybreak*

1992 *Slaughter* [Spur Award]

1994 *The Far Canyon* (Sequel to *Slaughter*) [Spur Award]

1996 *The Pumpkin Rollers*

1997 *Cloudy in the West*

1998 *Smiling Country* (Sequel to *The Good Old Boys*)

1999 *The Buckskin Line*

2001 *Badger Boy*

2001 *The Way of the Coyote* [Spur Award]

2002 *Ranger's Trail*

2004 *Texas Vendetta*

2004 *Jericho's Road*

2005 *Six Bits a Day* (Prequel to *The Good Old Boys*)

2008 *Hard Trail to Follow*

2008 *Many a River*

2009 *Other Men's Horses*

2010 *Texas Standoff* (Due October 2010)

(*First editions of these titles were paperback originals)

NONFICTION:

1972 *Looking Back West*
1981 *Frank C. McCarthy: The Old West*
1986 *Permian: A Continuing Saga*
1992 *Art of Frank C. McCarthy*
1992 *Art of Howard Terpning* [Western Heritage Award]
1992 *Living and Writing in West Texas*
1993 *Art of James Bama*
1993 *Elmer Kelton Country*
1993 *The Indian in Frontier News*
1995 *My Kind of Heroes*
1995 *Texas*
1999 *Texas Cattle Barons*
2003 *Christmas at the Ranch*
2007 *Sandhills Boy: The Winding Trail of a Texas Writer*

SHORT STORY COLLECTIONS:

1986 **The Big Brand*
1986 *There's Always Another Chance*

ADDITIONAL NOTES:

Lone Star Rising, Ranger's Law, Texas Sunrise, Texas Showdown, and *Brush Country* are not included in this checklist because they are omnibus reprints of Kelton's earlier novels.

The first editions of *Hot Iron* and *Buffalo Wagons* were simultaneously published in cloth. These limited hardback bindings were primarily for distribution to libraries and are quite scarce today.

Kelton wrote only the first three books in the *Sons of Texas* series under the publisher's "house" name of Tom Early. (Book four was by Frank Roderus; book five, Will C. Knott; book six, James Reasoner.)

The nine books in Kelton's *Texas Ranger Series* were published in this order:

Buckskin Line
Badger Boy
The Way of the Coyote
Ranger's Trail
Texas Vendetta
Jericho's Road
Hard Trail To Follow
Other Men's Horses
Texas Standoff

Kelton wrote three books under the pseudonym "Lee McElroy." He also wrote under two publisher's "house names": three books as "Tom Early;" and one book as "Alex Hawk."

Pecos Crossing (2008) is a reissue of *Horsehead Crossing*, originally published in 1963. *Shotgun* (2009) is a reissue of *Shotgun Settlement*, originally published in 1969 under the publisher's house name, Alex Hawk.

About the Contributors

Judy Alter

JUDY ALTER is former director of TCU Press and a longtime fan and friend of Elmer Kelton. She had worked on the TCU Press reprints of his books since 1984. She is the author of *Elmer Kelton and West Texas: A Literary Biography* (UNT Press) as well as the afterword to the TCU Press edition of *Wagontongue*.

Ricky Burk

DR. RICKY BURK has served as Senior Pastor of First United Methodist Church of San Angelo for four years. He was honored to be a friend of Elmer and privileged to deliver his eulogy at the funeral service which included "The Eyes of Texas" as an anthem and "Happy Trails" as the recessional.

Felton Cochran

FELTON COCHRAN lives in San Angelo, Texas. A longtime friend of Elmer's, he has owned and operated The Cactus Bookstore since 1995, site of many many successful signings of Elmer's books, new and old. On more than one occasion, Elmer told Felton his store was the largest single outlet for the sale of Elmer's titles.

Bob J. Frye

EMERITUS PROFESSOR OF ENGLISH BOB J. FRYE, in his forty-fourth year of teaching at TCU, was selected in 1996 to participate in the NEH Institute, "Integrating Curricula through Southwestern Studies" at Texas State University-San Marcos. That summer experience enabled him to offer two courses in Southwest American Literature and thus extend that tradition that Piper Professor Mabel Major initiated and Joyce Roach continued at TCU. He has been studying Elmer Kelton's work since 1983 and teaching Kelton and other Southwest writers since 1997 at TCU where he received the Chancellor's Award for Distinguished Teaching in

1992 and was named Texas Professor of the Year by the Carnegie Foundation in 1996.

Steve Kelton

STEVE KELTON is the son of Elmer and Anni Kelton. He was born and raised in San Angelo, where he lives today with his wife, Karen McGinnis. In his youth, he spent as much time as possible on the McElroy Ranch, managed by his grandfather, Buck Kelton, in Crane and Upton counties. He later spent twenty-five years on a ranch in Coke County before returning to San Angelo. Kelton has been with *Livestock Weekly* since 1977 and became its editor in 1994. He is the author of *Renderbrook, A Century Under The Spade Brand*, published in 1989 by TCU Press.

James Ward Lee

JAMES WARD LEE is emeritus professor of English and former chair of English at the University of North Texas. He is a past president and fellow of the Texas Folklore Society. Lee is the author of

Adventures with a Texas Humanist and, with Judy Alter, co-editor of *Literary Fort Worth*, both published by TCU Press.

Ruth McAdams

RUTH MCADAMS is professor of English and former chair of English at Tarrant County College, South Campus. Long a student and teacher of Elmer Kelton's work, she, along with James Ward Lee, interviewed Kelton for the Friends of the Fort Worth Public Library Evenings with Authors, and she wrote the afterword for the TCU Press reprint of *The Smiling Country*. Her most recent publications are chapters in *Grace & Gumption: Stories of Fort Worth Women* and *Grace & Gumption: The Cookbook*, TCU Press.

Joyce Roach

JOYCE ROACH is a TCU graduate, adjunct English faculty, author, folklorist, grassroots historian, and naturalist. She is a fellow of the Texas State Historical Association and the Texas Folklore Society, a member of both the Texas Institute of Letters and the Philosophical Society of Texas, president of the National Horned Lizard Conservation Society, director of the Center for Western Cross Timbers Studies, and an honoree in the National Cowgirl Museum and Hall of Fame. Elmer Kelton wrote an afterword to her book *The Cowgirls* (UNT Press), and she wrote an afterword for the TCU Press reprint of Kelton's *Honor at Daybreak*, 2002.